CULTURAL JOURNEYS

CULTURAL JOURNEYS:

84 Art and Social Science Activities From Around the World

Margaret W. Ryan

LP LEARNING PUBLICATIONS, INC.
Holmes Beach, Florida

Library of Congress Catalog in Publication Data

Ryan, Margaret W., 1922-
    Cultural journeys.

1. Art—Study and teaching (Elementary)—United States.
2. Art—Study and teaching (Secondary)—United States.
3. Intercultural education—United States. I. Title.

N362.R93 1989   700   88-45004

ISBN 1-55691-001-0 (pbk.)

Learning Publications, Inc.
5351 Gulf Drive
P.O. Box 1338
Holmes Beach, FL 34218

Cover and illustrations by author.

Printing: 6 5 4 3 2   Year: 5 4 3 2 1

Printed in the United States of America

ACKNOWLEDGMENTS

I would like first, to acknowledge the help of my husband, Dr. Douglas Ryan, for his invaluable aid in the research, writing and editing of this book and for his and my family's unflagging support of the project. Next, I would like to express my thanks for the support of my colleagues, the Art Department and the College of Fine Arts of the University of Southern Mississippi. My thanks to the editors of Learning Publications for their editorial help and the interest in the book. Lastly, but certainly not least, I would like to thank the students that helped me to test the projects and those who have expressed so much enthusiasm for the projects.

This book is dedicated to the teacher, art students and craftspeople who are always looking for something different to do and to those who have a great curiosity about how other people make things.

TABLE OF CONTENTS

INTRODUCTION

Cultural Journeys offers an opportunity to explore cultures of other places and times and to experience the thrill of creating original art works. These arts and crafts have been chosen from six continents and forty-three different countries. Sixteen of them are derived from the historical past.

Arts and crafts have been chosen as the focus of *Cultural Journeys* because visual and tactile perception is not bound by language or time barriers. Teachers and students can see and appreciate an art work while learning about the influences that made it a popular art form in its culture. The arts and crafts in these lessons were selected because they represent many ethnic styles. They are traditional techniques practiced by many people in a culture, not just by an individual artist or craftsman. Most of the arts and crafts chosen for *Cultural Journeys* have not been presented in other lessons on art or crafts.

These arts and crafts are unique because they depend upon the cultures and environments that produced them. In any culture, the economics, natural resources, level of civilization, trade or interaction with other groups, and beliefs of the people have an influence on the type of art expression produced. *Cultural Journeys* offers some insights into specific cases of these influences and points out how they coincide with, or differ from, those encountered in our own culture. These ideas can be used to enrich the curriculum.

The lessons in *Cultural Journeys* are designed to be taught by the classroom teacher. They have been received with enthusiasm by students of many age levels and have been recommended for use with the exceptional student.

Materials for these art and craft projects will provide a change from paper and pencil work. There is much emphasis on two dimensional art in the traditional curriculum; but, with the inclusion of ethnic crafts which usually have some practical use, three dimensional work makes up the major portion of *Cultural Journeys* lessons. The materials for these projects can often be had by collecting throw-aways or household materials. Sometimes, the materials used in the original cultures had to be changed because they are not available in most localities. For these materials, others have been substituted which can be obtained from local stores or through supply catalogues.

LESSON DESIGN

Lessons in *Cultural Journeys* are organized into sections of processes or materials that are similar. As an example, Section A deals with clay as a material and introduces several processes such as rolling, forming and carving clay. Section B is organized around weaving, twining and basket making. In Section C, the emphasis is on painting and drawing. Developing a unit around any of these sections will enable a teacher to build upon skills.

* The "A" level is designed for the student unfamiliar with the processes or materials.

* The "B" level projects require some planning and familiarity with simple tools.

* The "C" level lessons are more complex and, in some cases, more time consuming (may require several days).

Each lesson is a composite of seven basic divisions including:

* Historical and/or environmental background. This initial passage tells the background of the culture or the craft. It may also include notes on the making of the original project.

* Illustration of the art, craft or craftsperson in their original setting. Pictures are drawn from typical artifacts or people of the ethnic group.

* Social science concepts. Typical social science concepts are used that are appropriate for upper elementary through junior high school.

* Social science activities. The social science activities are designed to be answered not only from information in the beginning passage in the lesson, but also by referring to school atlases, encyclopedias, histories and social science texts. The activities are designed to provide motivation for further study and projects beyond the art project provided in the text.

* Art concept(s). The art lesson provides art concepts recognized in the field and coordinated with behavioral objectives.

* Art lesson plan. The lesson plan begins with an objective for student behavior. Also included are a list of materials which can be expanded to fit the size of the class. There is a step-by-step set of directions and, on some lessons, a note for further or different applications.

* Diagram or design example. The diagrams clarify the lesson instructions. Designs, when furnished, are examples of cultural motifs or for inspiration. However, students should be encouraged to study the characteristics of the design and to innovate on the theme.

These lessons in *Cultural Journeys* are designed to be used as an integrated experience. They may coordinate with art, civics, geography, history, social science and enhance the study of any of the relevant cultures. Teachers may wish to draw on the background of students who have experienced any of these arts or crafts.

SCOPE AND SEQUENCE:
SKILL INVENTORY

	Level - A	Level - B	Level - C
Additive Sculpture	5		
Baking/Firing	1, 2, 5	6, 7, 8, 9	10
Carving/Cutting	2, 3, 4, 20, 23, 30, 31, 45, 52, 63, 66, 74, 76	6, 7, 15, 26, 33, 35, 47, 57, 58, 69, 78, 79	27, 28, 29, 39, 50, 51, 72, 82, 83, 84
Casting/Molding	4, 22, 30		
Constructing	1, 2, 5, 22, 43, 55, 62, 63, 64, 65, 66	48, 56, 57, 58, 68, 69, 70, 78	10, 60, 71, 72, 80, 81
Dyeing	44	48	
Forming	1, 2, 76	6, 8, 59	10, 37, 60, 61
Incising/Piercing	32, 75	34, 77, 79	38, 39
Impressing/Bossing	32		36, 38, 39
Knotting/Tieing	12, 19	15, 24, 46, 56	27, 60
Loom Assembly			18
Painting	1, 2, 5, 22, 43, 53, 55, 63, 64, 65, 66	48, 56, 57, 58, 67, 68, 69, 70, 78	10, 60, 71, 72 78, 80
Pattern Making	43	47, 59	50, 60
Plaiting	20		28, 29
Plaster Moldmaking	3		61
Rolling	2, 3, 44	6, 9	11
Sewing	12, 14, 40, 41 42, 45, 66	46, 59	49, 51, 60, 83
Shredding		25	
Stenciling			73
Tile Setting		9	
Twining	12, 19, 31	17, 24	39
Warping/Weaving	13, 14	15, 16, 17, 35	18
Wax Gluing	21		

SCOPE AND SEQUENCE:
CONCEPT INVENTORY

Art Lessons	Level - A	Level - B	Level - C
Balance	2, 5, 40, 45, 54, 64	9, 34, 35, 69	60, 72, 81
Contrast/ Emphasis	19, 20, 21, 44, 53, 55, 64, 75	7, 16, 24, 26, 41, 47, 57, 68, 70, 77	10, 27, 50, 51, 61, 80
Dominance/Subord.	65, 40	56, 68, 77, 78	38, 62, 82
Dynamics (Movement)	3, 4, 42, 74, 76	17	10, 60
Harmony	43, 52, 65	8, 48, 78	36, 49, 62
Repetition	12, 14, 30, 32 42, 66	6, 15, 26, 46 58, 68, 79	18, 28, 36, 37, 50, 71, 80, 82, 83
Rhythm	20, 22, 31		29, 50
Simplification	2, 3, 12, 21, 32 45, 63, 67, 68	17, 33, 47, 70, 78, 79	36, 58, 61, 73, 82
Transition	13, 32	9, 67	38, 39
Unity	1, 12, 13, 22, 23, 30, 43, 55, 63	46, 48, 58, 59	10, 11, 49, 83
Variety	66	8, 25	84
Social Science Lessons			
Building	2, 20, 63	78	36
Communication	3, 63, 64, 65	6, 33	73
Culture	4, 5, 23, 32, 43, 64, 74	8, 17, 35, 48, 56, 58, 69, 78	10, 18, 27, 50, 60, 61, 72, 82
Economics	1, 14, 31, 54, 63, 65, 76	7, 25, 47	37, 39, 40, 49, 50, 51, 72, 81, 83
Geo./Resources	5, 12, 14, 21, 22, 40, 44, 45, 54, 66, 75	15, 16, 17, 22, 26, 46, 70	11, 28, 29, 62, 80, 84
History	1, 2, 4, 31, 42, 43	9, 33, 34, 47, 59	4, 36, 38
Households	14, 32, 44, 45, 55, 66, 76	9, 26, 47, 77	11, 18, 28, 37, 60, 62, 71, 80, 81, 83
Personal	22, 23, 30, 40, 41, 42, 43, 53	7, 24, 35, 46, 57	29, 37, 38, 39, 49, 50, 51, 82
Political	4, 41	58, 68	50, 62, 72
Religion/Rites	5, 30, 52, 53, 64	24, 57, 69, 78, 79	61, 73
Society	13, 19, 41, 55, 74	47, 48, 56, 71, 77	

1

HANDS, WHEELS AND ARMATURES

1. CHINESE ARTIFACTS (A)

In 1978, divers working in the Yellow Sea salvaged a rich cargo from the wreck of a trading vessel that had sunk with all hands aboard, more than six hundred and fifty years earlier. The treasure included more than 2,000,000 Chinese coins and 12,000 artifacts, among which were bronze and iron pots, weighing scales, and serving vessels. Also discovered were dishes, bowls, jugs and vases of stoneware, porcelain, and lacquer.

Of special interest were the wreck's many celadon pieces. Celadon is a high-fire ceramic stoneware that is glazed a soft, translucent green. Some pieces have a raised design. The celadon glaze flows off the object's high points and pools in its low ones to create a shaded effect. Much prized for its beautiful color transitions, celadon is called "ceramic jade." It was as treasured in the fourteenth century as it is today. Museums all over the world rank Chinese celadons among their most valued pieces.

SOCIAL SCIENCE EXPERIENCE

Concepts:

Value is determined by many criteria, such as rarity, aesthetics and cost of production.

Today, the real treasures of the deep are not only precious metals but also other kinds of artifacts from long ago.

Objectives:

To identify, observe and evaluate the factors that influence material values; to discuss such criteria as the age of an object; its rarity; its beauty; the amount of time/labor it took to produce it; the amount of cultural information it yields.

To develop research skills by surveying the many examples of ancient shipwrecks, then choosing one of them and locating as much data about it as possible.

Activities:

Search newspapers and magazines (*National Geographic, Treasure*) for news of recent treasure discoveries. Cross reference with accounts in other media.

Read and compare the opinions and aims of treasure hunters, collectors, archeologists.

View pictures/slides of recovered treasure.

Research the effects of the elements on various materials, especially sunken treasure.

ART EXPERIENCE

Concept:

A monochromatic color scheme can unify a complex piece.

Objectives:

To make, glaze and fire a pinch pot with rolled clay surface appliques.

To learn to maintain an even thickness in forming the wall of the pot.

To show relief and texture in applied designs.

To develop unity by using a monochromatic glaze.

To glaze one example in colors to compare with the effect of monochrome.

To view the inside of a kiln during firing (through a peephole, using protective glasses.)

To observe the color of heat.

Activity:

Materials: Ceramic clay, translucent glaze of medium value (green, rust, blue), a table knife, eaves, wooden sticks, brushes for glaze, a kiln.

Directions: Make a pinch pot 5" to 6" across, with walls not more than 1/2" thick. Trace leaf outlines onto rolled clay. Cut out the clay leaves, then moisten their backs and apply them to the surface of the pot. Make texture markings with a stick, a comb or a nail. Let the pot dry thoroughly, for about two weeks. Then, use a brush to generously apply three coats of glaze. Dry between coats and before firing (at temperature stated on the glaze jar). Stilt glazed ware to prevent drips on the kiln shelf.

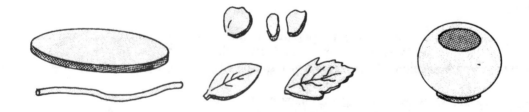

2.   MINOAN HOUSE FACADE (A)

The Minoan civilization, one of the world's earliest cultures, flourished on the island of Crete in the eastern Mediterranean from about 3000 to 1100 B.C. Knossos, its greatest city, had beautiful palaces, an efficient road system and functioning sewers. It was the most modern of the time. Minoan ships dominated the Aegean and Mediterranean seas.

But suddenly, in 1450 B.C., at the height of its power, the Minoan empire collapsed. Some scholars believe that the cause of the downfall was a massive volcanic eruption on the nearby island of Thera which was accompanied by earthquakes, tidal waves, and the fall of poisonous ash on Crete.

The Minoan empire was unable to recover its former glory, and finally disappeared about 1100 B.C. Little exists in the way of written records with which to reconstruct the history and culture of the Minoans. However, archeologists have discovered an abundance of architecture, painting, sculpture, pottery, jewelry, and other material remains of this great Bronze Age culture. Among these, Minoan ceramic artifacts are judged the most important and reliable resources available today for the study of ancient cultures.

Among the artifacts found at Knossos were miniature ceramic plaques depicting the fronts of Minoan homes. Dubbed by archeologists "The Town Mosaics," they are thought to represent the actual appearance and arrangement of houses along a Minoan street of long ago. The plaques reveal in great detail such ancient architectural features as: the types of materials used in construction; the use of windowless walls at street level; and the appearance of Minoan doors, windows, sills, and overhanging eaves.

Originally, the small, tile-like Minoan house plaques may have been decorative inlays from a chest or other piece of furniture. They were produced using the "faience" technique, which results in a ceramic material that is durable and almost impervious to weather. To make faience, the pottery is painted with a colored clay underglaze, then the piece is bisque-fired, glazed again and, finally, fired again.

SOCIAL SCIENCE EXPERIENCE

Concept:

Many interdependent systems are necessary to support large, complex populations. Early cities, as well as those of today, can be evaluated in terms of the quality of their buildings, roads, water and sewer systems.

Objectives:

To identify reasons why civilizations rise and fall.

To detail the reasons why certain early civilizations had such success. To identify the characteristics of systems in early civilizations. Compare them with the characteristics of systems. in a modern city.

Activities:

Locate Crete on a map. Research its present political, economic and cultural situation.

Study the floor plans and reconstructions of the palace at Knossos.

Read the legend of King Minos and discuss how stories about the lives of ancient kings and heroes pass into myth. Compare the stories of King Arthur, the kings of Troy, and others.

Research and discuss the effects of natural disasters on the ancient world. Compare the downfall of the dinosaurs; the myth of Atlantis; the remains at Pompeii.

ART EXPERIENCE

Concept:

A frontal image shows shape without perspective.

Objectives:

To make plaques showing the facades of students' homes; or, to make a series of plaques depicting the fronts of buildings on a local street.

To simplify three-dimensional features into two-dimensional shapes.

To develop skill in rolling, carving, painting and glazing clay.

To learn the process of firing.

Activity:

Materials: Ceramic clay, underglazes, clear glaze, a rolling pin, a pair of 1/4" slats, a table knife, straws, soft brushes for glaze, a kiln.

Directions: Make a drawing of a building's facade, allowing two inches per floor. Show its windows, door and roof. Cut out the shape of the building. Using 1/4" slats to control thickness, roll out clay on a flat surface that has been "floured" with dry clay. Trace the shape of the building onto the rolled clay and trim off the excess. Use a straw to pierce holes in the clay (for hanging the plaque). Use clay rolling, carving, and incising techniques to add details, such as the textures of the building's construction materials. Paint the plaque with underglaze colors, then fire and cool. Apply three coats of clear glaze to the front of the plaque and fire again.

3. PHAISTOS DISK OF CRETE (A)

Pictures are the oldest and most universal form of written communication. Even people who speak different languages can understand information that is presented in picture form.

Throughout history primitive people of all races have developed and used many different kinds of picture languages to record information. The picture-symbols used in these communication systems are called "pictographs." The earliest histories of the Egyptians, Babylonians, Chinese and native Americans were recorded in pictographs on stone, wood or clay.

Modern children in the early-learning years enjoy reading books that use a form of pictograph called a "rebus," in which a picture represents a word or a syllable. By recognizing a combination of picture symbols, such as a picture of a bee, followed by the letter "N," followed by a picture of some ice cubes, a child can "read" the message, "Bee" "n" + "ice," as "Be nice."

In 1900 A.D., the Phaistos Disc, a clay disc covered with pictographs, was found among the remains of the Minoan palace at Phaistos, on Crete. The disc is thought to date from before 1700 B.C. Its pictographs are unique because they were not inscribed by hand. Instead, they are pressed into the clay with special stamps. The Phaistos Disc, therefore, is one of the earliest examples of printed matter. Its surface displays a spiral column divided into 61 spaces, which bear 241 different pictographs made from combinations of 36 stamps.

Even today, with all of the technologically advanced decoding methods that are currently available, the Phaistos Disc still has not been deciphered entirely.

SOCIAL SCIENCE EXPERIENCE

Concepts:

Cultures devise methods to keep information in the form of records.

Written language develops as cultures grow increasingly complex.

Objectives:

To consider the kinds of information that people in a culture must all share in order for the culture to survive.

To provide experience in coding language into pictorial symbols.

To compare today's written language with written languages in ancient messages.

Activities:

Find examples of and study other pictographic systems: Egyptian hieroglpyhs, Mayan pictographs, international road signs, Victorian rebuses and others.

Study other undeciphered languages: Etruscan.

Create rebuses.

ART EXPERIENCE

Concepts:

Lines create movement in design.

Pictures can carry definite verbal meanings.

Objectives:

To make a pictograph disc.

To simplify pictorial symbols into designs for stamps.

To create a visual path with a spiraling line to direct the reading of stamped symbols.

To develop skills in rolling, molding, carving and making appliques.

Activity:

Materials: Plaster of Paris, small plastic bottle caps, a non-stick baking pan spray, a bowl, ceramic clay, a nail or gouge, wax paper, a rolling pin, a pair of wooden slats (1/4" thick).

Directions: Design a short rebus message using nouns and action verbs.   Make stamps for each pictograph in the rebus by spraying plastic caps with non-stick coating, filling them with plaster, and when dry, carving pictographs into their plaster surfaces.   Next, using slats to maintain an even thickness, roll the clay into a disc about 12" in diameter. (Pierce a hole in the top of the disc, if it is to be hung.)   In the bowl, use water to thin some clay to the consistency of runny icing.   Pour the thinned clay into a cone made of wax paper, cut off the tip of the cone and direct its contents onto the clay disc, drawing a spiral line.   Maintain a distance of 1" (or more) between the lines of the spiral.   Next, to make pictographs, press 1/2" balls of clay onto the plaster stamps and trim the edges.   Remove the flattened clay balls from the stamps.   Apply thinned clay to their backs and place them between the lines on the disc.   Begin the message at the center of the spiral and work outward.   Draw vertical lines to indicate pauses. Allow to dry and then fire.

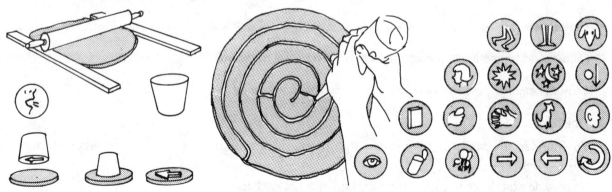

4.   SANDSTONE STATUES OF PERSEPOLIS (A)

Waiting for centuries at the ruined palace of ancient Persepolis, a procession of stone men climbs the wide staircase leading to the king's audience chamber. Each man is a silent envoy bearing a gift in tribute to Darius I, king of Persia from 521 to 486 B.C. The almost endless line of stone tributaries was intended to remind human viewers of the power and grandeur of Persepolis and its kings. The reminder is as effective today as it was when first created.

Persepolis, the ceremonial capital of Persia, was a magnificent symbol of the power of the Persian rulers, until Alexander the Great of Greece defeated the city in 331 B.C. and burned it to the ground. While his men pillaged the land, Alexander married the daughter of Darius III and took command of the two kingdoms.

The relief carvers of ancient Persia who sculpted the sandstone gift bearers were mindful of the boredom of waiting. Some of the figures stand with one foot resting on the next step. Others turn back to look at their neighbors. Two of the figures cover their mouths with their hands, as if to stifle yawns. A few reach out and touch the men ahead of them, as if to call for their attention.

The soft beige sandstone from which the figures were sculpted was easily shaped with a sanding technique. The finished figures are rounded, and their features are stylized rather than naturalistic. Dressed in the clothing representative of their many homelands, the men still stand waiting in their 2500-year-long line, with no end in sight.

SOCIAL SCIENCE EXPERIENCE

Concept:

Monumental sculpture and architecture are physical proof of their builder's command of material wealth and labor. They are symbols of power.

Objectives:

To identify the types of structures, monuments and institutions that can represent power.

To recognize and analyze the probable motives of monument builders and sculpture commissioners.

Activities:

Identify the times when contemporary people wait in line. Pantomime some of the typical postures they assume.

Compare the types and purposes of monuments such as the palace at Persepolis, the Lincoln monument, Notre Dame de Paris, the World Trade Center, the arch in St. Louis, the Corn Palace in Mitchell, S.D., others.

Imagine standing in line to see Darius I. What topics would the people discuss?

Visit the most powerful public building in your community. Discuss its age, materials, the source of the money used to finance its construction and the time and labor involved in its construction.

ART EXPERIENCE

Concept:

Variations in figures rendered in profile create interest and a sense of movement in relief sculpture.

Objectives:

To sculpt a frieze of figures in profile, all moving in one direction.

To vary the position of the figures' arms and legs to add interest and movement to the frieze.

To gain unity with repetition of textures and forms.

To acquire skill in making a plaster cast and carving in reverse.

Activity:

Materials: A shoe box, plaster of Paris, dry color (ochre) to make beige, white glue, sand, a bucket, a plastic knife, tablespoons, wax paper, nails, paper clips, water.

Directions: Mix plaster in a bucket. Color the plaster sandy-beige by adding a teaspoon or two of dry color. Line the shoe box with waxed paper and pour in 1 1/2" of plaster. Tap the outside of the box to remove air bubbles. Let the plaster dry overnight and remove it from the box. Draw a row of 4" figures in profile on the plaster. Scrape away 1/2" of the background, leaving the figures raised above the plaster surface. Shape the raised figures, rounding them and adding textures. When finished, coat the plaster with glue and sprinkle with sand (for a sandstone texture).

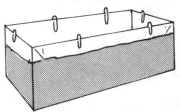   

5.   CLAY FIGURES OF ACHMICHO (A)

Mexican potters are quick to set up shop wherever they find a supply of natural clay, usually in or near a river. They set up their kilns nearby, and fire clay figures at fairly low temperatures. (Only ceramic ware intended for cooking is fired at high temperatures.) After cooling, the figures are decorated with paint or lacquer.

The Tarascan Indians who live in the village of Achmicho in western Mexico make clay figures which depict subjects drawn from daily life: workers, animals, dancers, clowns. Other favorite subjects represent the fantasies, fears and superstitions of the people, as well as spirits from the underworld. The subjects vary widely. One piece may show Eve wrestling with the snake in the Garden of Eden; another may show gleeful demons doing a fanciful dance. Fantastic monsters are a special favorite. However, far from being terrifying and fearsome, the figures are brightly colored and festive, and show a great deal of action and expression.

SOCIAL SCIENCE EXPERIENCE

Concept:

Objects can be used to represent otherwise intangible concepts and emotions.

Objectives:

To recognize and identify some of the messages that are conveyed by symbols and symbolic objects.

To recognize the universal human practice of substituting symbolic objects and entities to serve as surrogates for real problems and fears.

Activity:

Make a list of symbolic characters or objects presented in print and television advertising: soil-gobbling enzymes, warriors against tooth decay, and other symbolic creatures. Explain their purposes.

Discuss the meaning of the word, "scapegoat." Find examples of scapegoats throughout history.

Research and then write/perform a radio play depicting a supernatural being's effect on a town. Use description and sound effects.

ART EXPERIENCE

Concept:

Three-dimensional balance revolves around a central core.

Objective:

To construct papier mache' figures on an armature.

Activity:

Materials: Newspaper, wallpaper paste, a container, string, a wooden stick, nails, a hammer, a wooden block, enamel paints, lacquer, and brushes.

Directions: Nail the end of the stick to the center of the block.   Use wet newspaper to form the shape of the figure around the stick.   Wrap and tie the shape with string to prevent the paper from loosening as it dries.   (Make sure that the figure is balanced and will not fall over.)   Let dry for one or two days.   Mix water with wallpaper paste in the container.   Cover the figure with strips of newspaper dipped in the paste.   Keep the surface smooth and build the features to show character. Dry thoroughly. Paint to bring out character.

(The model may be covered with clay and fired as an alternate method.)

6.   SUMERIAN CYLINDER SEALS (B)

For the most of the third millennium B.C. the Sumerian civilization dominated the fertile area between the Tigris and the Euphrates Rivers in southern Mesopotamia (present-day Iraq). Sumer's power was based to a large extent on its development of irrigated agriculture.   The Sumerians are also noted for their art work and metallurgy, cuneiform writing, and the provision for past, present and future tense forms in their language.

The necessities of trade and a strong sense of property contributed to the development of a Sumerian system of phonetic writing which assigned specific symbols to specific sounds and allowed the Sumerians to record any language, even if they couldn't understand it.

A Sumerian contract was written on a moist clay tablet and then wrapped in a thin envelope of more moist clay.   The contract was written a second time on the outside of the envelope.   To authenticate their contracts, the Sumerians developed special kinds of seals. Their designs were engraved into stone or fired clay cylinders.   When rolled across the envelope, the various cylinder seals made positive impressions.   Each was unique to its owner.   If a dispute about the terms of the contract arose, the seal designs would confirm the contractors' identities. Also, the outer clay envelope could be chipped off to reveal the terms of the original agreement.

Artists were hired to engrave cylinder seals with designs representing types of businesses, significant events or scenes from mythology.   Sumerian businessmen wore their seals around their necks, suspended on leather thongs.

SOCIAL SCIENCE EXPERIENCE

Concepts:

Language develops as cultures grow more complex.

Cultures invent ways to record information and keep records.

Accurate records must be kept of contracts, trade agreements and other documents.

Objectives:

To identify the reasons why contracts are made; explain their purposes.

To identify the various levels of making trade or business agreements.   Rank them from least to most complex in terms of their rules and the obligations of their parties.

Activities:

List current practices in the authentification of documents (public notaries, witnesses, signatures, seals et cetera).

Research the parts of a contract (parties, definitions, items, considerations, time factors and other limitations).

Describe various types of contracts and agreements: service, marriage, deed, bank loan, bill of sale, performance, Students Against Drunk Driving (SADD), and others.

Write a sample contract between two students, a student and a parent, or students and a teacher.

Invite an attorney to talk about parent's responsibilities and liabilities regarding offspring in your state. What is the law if a minor signs an agreement to purchase a magazine subscription, for example? If parents sign a waiver so their child can take a class trip, and the child is injured?

ART EXPERIENCE

Concept:

Relief designs inked and mounted on cylinders can produce endless repetitions of themselves.

Objectives:

To make a relief design cylinder.

To design a relief motif for mounting on a cylinder; with no beginning or ending point.

To learn to carve an interacting design (with no beginning or end) on a cylinder. When inked and rolled on a surface, the carved cylinder will print out infinitely repeated versions of the design it bears.

To develop skill in clay-rolling, carving and kiln-stacking.

Activity:

Materials: Moist clay, a "bobby pin," a paper clip, a pencil, a kiln.

Directions: Roll the clay out to a thickness of 1/2". Cut a clay strip 2" wide. Form the strip around a pencil, trim the excess, smooth the seam and remove the pencil. Let the cylinder dry to leather hard. Straighten out a paper clip. Use it to draw and incise a design around the cylinder. Remember to carve the design in reverse (with a bobby pin). Dry the cylinder. (Stack the dry cylinders in the kiln, on end, 1/4" to 1/2" apart, and fire.) Impress the finished cylinder's design by firmly rolling it on a moist clay surface.

 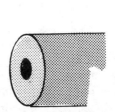 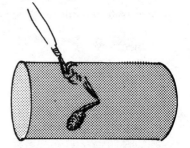

7.   BEADS OF OMAN   (B)

Oman is a sultanate of approximately 82,000 square miles in southeastern Arabia. Comprised mainly of a narrow coastal plain and a dry interior plateau, Oman is dwarfed geographically and economically by its much larger neighbor, Saudi Arabia. Both countries share a common ancestry derived from the Persians and Asiatics who settled the enormous sandy peninsula that is shared by their countries. Likewise, both possess large and extremely valuable oil reserves.

Oman was once the most important state in Arabia due to its dominant location on the Gulf of Oman and its ports on the Arabian Sea. Before Oman's oil industry was developed, dates were its major export.

In spite of the wealth which oil has brought to Oman, the people maintain their traditional customs and dress. One such tradition, the display of personal wealth by wearing it, has persisted among Oman's families.

Women in Oman hoard silver and wear it as evidence of their personal or family wealth. It is usually seen in the form of strung silver beads, an easily carried domestic treasure. Varying in size and shape—barrels, rounds, and bugles, with incised designs—many beads are very old and appear to be well-rubbed and worn from constant handling.

SOCIAL SCIENCE EXPERIENCE

Concept:

The accumulation and display of wealth is present in most cultures and takes many forms.

Objectives:

To find evidence of the various ways that wealth can be acquired: trade, inheritance, dowry, reparations, and theft which are displayed as jewelry, and specific possessions.

To compare the custom in Oman and the custom in monarchies in which royal jewelry is collected and worn; also, the custom in private families of accumulating jewelry; also, determine other examples.

Activities:

Discuss "ostentation."

Identify the latest form(s) of ostentatious display among contemporary youth.

Research "potlatch" activities among Northwest American natives. Are there any parallels between potlatch activities and human behavior in other relationships?

Debate the features/benefits/negative aspects of communal property vs. personal property ownership.

ART EXPERIENCE

Concept:

Contrasts in color, size, texture and base material can relieve monotony in a piece.

Objectives:

To make a necklace.

To develop skills in rolling cylinders, cutting and carving in clay.

To learn to vary forms of beads, (barrels, rounds, bugles) to gain emphasis.

To experience arranging beads in various configurations to achieve symmetry/asymmetry, balance, imbalance, and harmony/disharmony.

Activity:

Materials: Self-hardening clay or salt dough (2 C. flour, 1 C. salt, 1/2 C. water), paper clips, a hair pin, colored beads, a nail, 24" of wire (stiff), silver paint, a knife.

Directions: Determine the desired length of the necklace and the number and sizes of the beads to be made. Mark these sizes on paper for reference. Mix clay. Roll out a "snake" of clay. Make its thickness correspond to the desired diameter of the beads. Use the knife to cut off bead-sized pieces (in pairs, for left/right symmetry). Work matching beads at the same time; cover to keep moist. Use a nail to pierce through the center of the clay (to make the stringing hole), then incise the bead surfaces. Make a larger-sized bead for the center of the necklace. Finish making all of the beads and put them aside to dry. Bake. Spray with silver paint. Alternate silver and colored beads to make a symmetrical pattern (exactly the same on each side of the center).

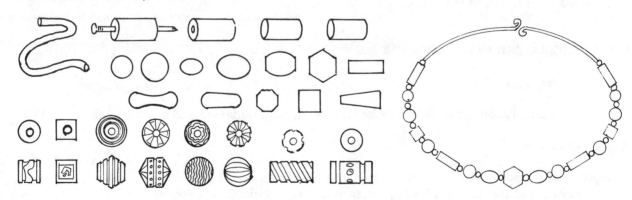

8.   INCA GENRE POTTERY OF PERU (B)

Peru is one of the world's archeological treasure chests.   More than 500 years ago, the rich cultures of the Nazca, Chimor, Chaven, Mochican and Paracan tribes came under the domination of the Inca civilization.   The cultural products of each tribe blended with and enhanced the others, resulting in a highly sophisticated level of craft production in many different media.

This is readily apparent in the influence of Mochican and Nazca ceramics on Inca genre (everyday) pottery pieces.   Practical and not crude, the Inca pieces display great technical skill and a pleasing simplicity of design. Subjects are drawn from the daily lives of the Incas.   They show the character of their people and their homes, their occupations, commonplace tasks, recreational activities, significant animals and their myths.   Inca pottery pieces might show Incas doing anything, from painting a house to taking a mud bath.

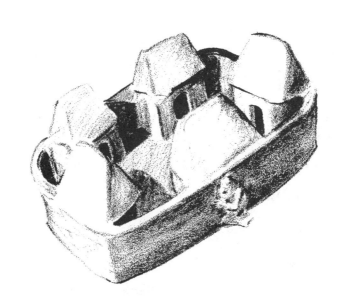

Peruvian genre pieces are made of clay and fired.   They are made in many styles, from realistic to abstract, and can serve many purposes, from humorous to serious.

SOCIAL SCIENCE EXPERIENCE

Concept:

Genre artifacts may (or may not) provide an accurate representation of the life styles of the people who fabricated them.

Objectives:

To consider both the practical and the aesthetic reasons for artisans in a culture to make genre pottery.

To compare standardized products to unique (one of a kind) products.   Cite the positive and the negative attributes of each.

To identify the tools and techniques used by scientists to evaluate the qualities of ancient regalia.

To observe the kinds of evidence used to develop a hypothesis concerning an ancient culture.

Activities:

Identify objects in contemporary homes (a cartoon character night lamp) and in the community (a gasoline station sign logo) that bear figurative decorations (especially decorations in relief).

Identify story-telling objects/artifacts by their categories, such as mythological, religious, political or others.

ART EXPERIENCE

Concept:

Three-dimensional genre design can be applied to functional uses.

Objectives:

To use the form of a person, bird or animal as the body of a clay vessel (dish, cup, vase). Have the head, wings or paws serve as a decorative lid or handles or a base.

To integrate disparate forms to make a unified piece.

To gain skill in making a coil or pinch pot.

To learn to stack a kiln.

Activity:

Materials: Ceramic clay, smoothing tools, a kiln

Directions: Choose an everyday subject: a house, an animal, a car or a person. Simplify the detail. Form the basic shape with clay coils and/or slabs. (Clay thicker than 1/2" can not be fired, so the pieces must be hollow.) Add details and let dry to leather-hard. Then, polish the figure with fingers, and fire it when it is completely dry. Unglazed ware may be stacked on shelves or at the bottom of the kiln without stilts. Pieces may touch each other (although it is better if they do not).

9.   STORYTELLING MOSAICS OF TUNISIA (B)

Modern Tunis, the capital city of Tunisia, stands upon the ruins of other ancient cities. First to be built on the site, in the 9th century B.C., was the Phoenician city of Carthage which grew in power and wealth until it rivaled Rome.   Later, both cities fought the Punic wars, a series of three wars which took place over a hundred year period.   At the end of the third Punic war, in 146 B.C., Carthage was destroyed.   Later, in 44 B.C., the Roman victors built a city on the ruins.   Near present day Tunis is another ruin of the town that housed Roman soldiers who guarded the city from the South.   This was Thyschyus which is now called Eljem.

Today Thyschyus is the site of archeological exploration.   The baths and other buildings have yielded lively mosaics which show scenes from Roman mythology (such as the voyage of Ulysses), the sports of the Colosseum, and the delights of a luxurious Roman lifestyle.

Originally, both the walls and the floors were decorated with mosaics.   However, most of the wall mosaics are gone, their stones taken away to be used elsewhere.   But the floors are largely intact.   Their designs are composed of small tiles of fired clay, about 1/2" square, in earthy colors of brown, white, yellow, tan and rust.   Shapes in the designs are outlined in dark tiles, then filled in with other appropriate colors and shaded in rows at the edges to create the effect of modeling and volume.

SOCIAL SCIENCE EXPERIENCE

Concept:

Much can be learned about other cultures through the study of utilitarian objects and genre artifacts.   Utilitarian objects often serve to present and preserve the myths, stories and values of a culture.

Objectives:

To consider and compare the qualities of functional objects vs. decorative objects.

To explore the concept of "trade-off" (or compromise), as a consideration in the design of a building.

Activities:

Study the mosaics of the Romans, the Byzantines (at Ravenna) and Antonio Gaudi.

List and discuss the transitory nature of decoration fads, now and in various other historic time periods.

ART EXPERIENCE

Concept:

Shape reads as form when shading is added.

Objectives:

To create a mosaic in earth colors.

To use shading to lend volume to shapes.

To create transitions in color values to make shading.

To develop skill in setting tile.

To consider the differences between design that is applied to a surface and design that is assembled.

Activity:

Materials: Floor tiles (soft plastic or composition) in earth colors, glue, plaster of Paris, thin plywood (for backing), a bucket, shears, a spreader (for glue).

Directions: Cut tiles into 1/4" squares. On a board, draw a simple design showing shapes and background. Edge the light side of each design shape with tiles in the lightest color. Edge the shadow side of the shape with tiles of the darkest shade. Begin putting rows of the lightest tones next to the lightest color tiles and shade the shape (by using increasingly darker shaded tiles) from there to the edge of the darkest outline. Place tiles about 1/16" apart. After the tiles for each shape are tested in place, glue them onto the board. Mix only a little plaster at a time (use about 3 tbsp. with a very little water). Work plaster paste around the edges of the tiles and use a damp cloth to wipe their surfaces clean as each area is finished. (Fired clay may be used instead of tiles.)

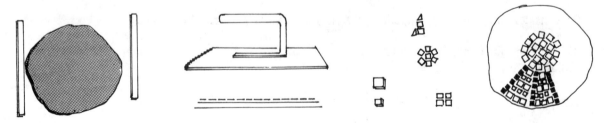

10. GREEK ACTION POTTERY (C)

When there is no written history, a primary source of information about a civilization is its artifacts. In the case of Greece, the most plentiful and characteristic artifacts are examples of painted and engraved pottery.

Around 1000 B.C. it was the fashion to decorate Greek pottery with geometric designs. Later, these decorations began to be replaced by drawings showing people or groups of animals in profile. Soon the drawings were made to depict actions or to show events in the Greek world. Gradually, as contact with Ionia (a neighbor to the East) increased, the drawn figures became even more graceful and realistic.

Around 550 B.C., at Ceramicus on the outskirts of Athens, another style of pottery, called the "black figure," came into popularity. In this technique the pottery was light buff colored and the figures painted on it were black. Then, when dry, details were scratched through the black surface to expose the light base color that had been hidden below (sgraffito technique).

Styles changed again and the background became black, with figures painted on it in light clay colors using free brush strokes. Other colors of clay were sometimes added to the design. This development was accompanied by more attention to the composition of the figures in relation to the shape of the pot or jug. The figures were drawn in profile and the action that they showed led the eye around the piece in either a clockwise or counter-clockwise direction.

Another important development was the invention of mold-making. Because it enabled potters to make multiples of their products, faster and easier, this innovation greatly expanded trade, not only in pottery, but also in other kinds of commodities that could be carried in pots.

SOCIAL SCIENCE EXPERIENCE

Concepts:

Pottery decorations provide important evidence for tracing the contacts between early cultures.

The production methods of products have an effect on the expansion of markets.

Objectives:

To recognize the influences of various cultures on one's own culture.

To find out how the production of products changes to meet the demands of expanding business.

Activities:

Visit a local supermarket. Observe examples of the variety of food products and the different cultures that they represent.

Visit a local manufacturing plant. Find out how the management deals with research, product development, production efficiency and marketing.

Use a library's magazine archives to research the changes which have occurred in the last fifty years for any of the following: clothing fashion, automobiles, appliances, toys, home entertainment.

ART EXPERIENCE

Concepts:

Design stands out if the foreground value is opposite that of the background value (positive/negative, light/dark, dark/light).

Figures in profile, all facing the same way, create a sense of flow or direction in a design.

Objectives:

To make a decorated clay bowl.

To contrast the value used in decorative figures with the value used in the background for the figures.

To create a unified sense of movement or action through presenting figures facing in the same direction.

To improve skill in stacking and firing a kiln.

Activity:

Materials: Clay, paper, a bowl, a rolling pin, a pair of 1/4" wooden slats, a clay scraper and trimmer, a cloth, a sponge, a brush, underglaze in two contrasting values.

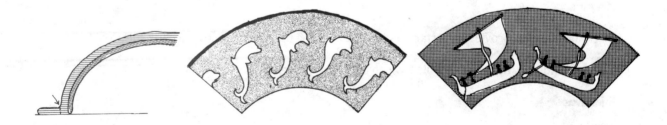

Directions: Turn the bowl upside down and cover it with wet paper strips; keep the surface smooth. On the cloth, roll out a clay circle between the slats. Place the bowl on the center of the clay. Put a hand under the cloth and lift clay and cloth, turning them over into the bowl. Remove the cloth and press the clay to conform to the bowl's shape. Trim the edges. Let the clay dry until leather-hard. Remove the dry bowl-shaped clay from the bowl and discard the paper. Let the clay bowl dry. Measure its circumference and divide it into several sections; have each section be large enough to show a drawing of a figure in profile. Because of the contour of the bowl, the figures will have less space at their bottoms than at their tops. Therefore, taper the design for each figure. Designs on paper can be transferred easily by cutting out the figures and stenciling them onto the bowl with the first coat of underglaze. Apply three layers of underglaze and then fire. If a waterproof finish is desired, glaze the bowl and refire.

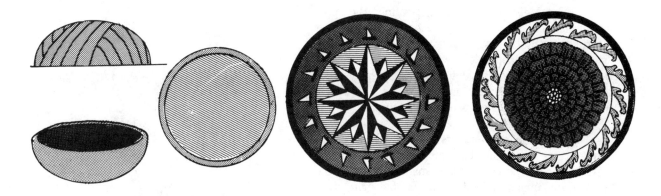

11. GENRE POTTERY OF GUATEMALA (C)

The ancient Mayan Indians lived in the uplands of Guatemala, western Honduras and parts of Mexico. Their culture flourished from the first millennium B.C. to the Spanish conquest of Central America in the mid-sixteenth century. They are noted for their magnificent sculpture and architecture, their remarkably accurate calendar and their advanced systems of writing, mathematics and astronomy.

Like the ancient Greeks, the Maya developed many independent city-states rather than one centralized government. The city-states were bound together under the rule of an intellectual priesthood. The Maya were landowners who worked cooperatively to sow and harvest grain.

Archeologists are still excavating the pre-Columbian cities of the Maya. Among their most informative finds have been examples of Maya "genre" pottery featuring a wide variety of subjects from everyday life. Besides cups, pots and vessels, the Maya made pottery in the shapes of flutes, whistles, fruit, vegetables, people and animals.

Today, the descendants of the Maya retain some of the traditions of their ancestors. Pottery in the Mayan style is still being made in Guatemala. It is fired unglazed and then painted with very bright colors. Later, the pottery is covered with several coats of lacquer to achieve a shiny gloss. Most of the pieces are purely decorative.

SOCIAL SCIENCE EXPERIENCE

Concepts:

Archeologists can learn a great deal about an ancient culture from its utilitarian objects.

People living in security can produce decorative objects.

Decorated pottery can function as a device to spread the myths, stories and values of a culture.

Objectives:

To identify the purposes for the creation and use of genre pottery (by the Maya, as well as by other cultures).

To identify the changing roles of the hand-made vs. the mass-produced, the permanent vs. the disposable.

Activities:

Observe and deduce information about a culture based on a piece of pottery produced by it. Cite examples such as an ancient Egyptian cat, Achmicho pottery, English Toby jugs, others.

Identify and enumerate the purposes of the decorations on contemporary utilitarian objects: Spiderman plastic cups, rock star T-shirts, logos of all types, and others.

Discuss how everyday objects can shed light on ancient cultures and customs. Answer questions such as: How was a piece of pottery used? to hold wine? Beer? Milk? Did the people who made/used it have permanent dwellings to decorate/embellish? Did they have leisure time to enjoy such embellishment? A sense of humor?

Imagine an excavation of your room at home by future archeologists. What could they infer from their findings?

ART EXPERIENCE

Concept:

Similar subjects, shapes and forms can unify a work.

Objectives:

To make a genre wreath.

To develop unity by using similar elements.

To show proportionate size relationships.

To develop skill in forming dough.

Activities:

Materials: Salt-dough (flour - 3 C., salt - 1 C., water - 1 C.), extra flour, a rolling pin, a table knife, paint, lacquer or plastic coating.

Directions: Mix bread dough in a bowl and work on a floured surface. Roll out the dough in a circle, 1/2" thick and 12" in diameter. Cut out a wreath shape. Make a hole for hanging. Shape fruit, vegetable and leaf forms. Use water (as glue) to attach the forms to the wreath shape. Add leaves until the shape is covered. Bake in the oven for 2 hours at 250° F. (until dough begins to brown). Paint, lacquer or apply a plastic coating.

2

WARPS, WEFTS, SPINDLES AND KNOTS

12. SALISH BASKETS (A)

Many diverse and unique crafts originated among the Indians of northwestern North America. The Chilkat tribe is renowned for its twined blankets; the Haida peoples are known for their totems and bear, wolf and deer masks; and the Hamatsos, Nootkas and Loolaxo tribes for their animal and demon motif sculptures.

Equally impressive is the reputation as accomplished weavers and basketmakers that has been earned by the Salish Indians of western Montana. The Salish have made a creative and practical use of the somewhat limited resources to be found in their environment. Their blankets, for example were woven from a combination of mountain goat wool, rabbit fluff and dog's hair. In fact, they raised dogs and sheared their heavy hair to use in spinning yarn to weave blankets.

Salish basketweavers use a coiling method and flat bundles of fibers or reeds to make the sides of their baskets. The first coils are usually started from a wooden bottom, then sewn together rather than twined or plaited. The finished baskets have flat sides that taper outward and upward. Their decoration consists of geometric patterns.

SOCIAL SCIENCE EXPERIENCE

Concepts:

To satisfy the demand for valued objects or commodities, artisans in a culture may create imitations, or many variations on a theme.

To produce the imitations, the artisans may employ other, unusual materials or innovative techniques that are more efficient or less expensive.

Objectives:

To recognize the differences between originals and copies.

To find positive/negative qualities in originals. To find positive/negative qualities in copies.

To identify the variety of reasons why people make substitutes for valued items.

Activities:

Collect three examples of "imitation" materials and bring them to class. Discuss whether the original material is too costly, too time-intensive or obsolete.

Find examples of trompe l'oeil fine and decorative artworks in: Napoleonic France, Renaissance Italy and colonial America.

Discuss the imitation of materials in our own culture: plastic laundry baskets that look like woven fibers; faux marble bathroom counters; linoleum tiles that look like fired clay; synthetic fabrics that imitate silk, velvet, fur; metal desks that look like wood; jeweled studs on blue jeans jackets; buttons that look like bone or mother-of-pearl.

ART EXPERIENCE

Concepts:

Repetition unifies design. Graduated shapes unify form.

Coiling is an alternative to plaiting and twining in basket weaving.

Objectives:

To coil weave a small oblong basket.

To gain unity through the repetition of geometric design and the graduation of shape.

Activity:

Materials: Heavy cardboard, raffia (or 1/2"-wide plastic sheeting strips, yarn needle).

Directions: From cardboard, cut a basket bottom (in an elliptical shape) with a lengthwise slot in the center. Cut 1" wide strips of cardboard in lengths suitable for forming four layers of the basket's sides. Use raffia strips or plastic strips (cut from plastic bags or sheeting). Thread a raffia strand (or a plastic strip) through the yarn needle. Pass the raffia strand through the slit in the basket bottom and completely wrap the bottom. (Replace the strand, as needed, by overlapping the tail end of the old strand with the front end of the new one.) Attach the first cardboard basket side to the bottom piece by stitching each side wrap through a wrap on the bottom piece, all the way around. Add second, third, and fourth sides the same way. (To finish the ends of the cardboard side strips, overlap them and wrap around the double thickness.) Use contrasting raffia or plastic strips to create a design in the wrapping.

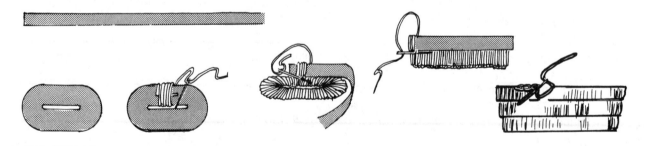

13. IKAT WALL HANGINGS (A)

Ikat is an ancient dye-resist technique that is still practiced today, especially in Indonesia. In order to produce an Ikat wall hanging, weft yarn strands are bound together with string or fibre at definite intervals in a deliberate pattern. Wherever the strands are tied, the dye is prevented from penetrating. After drying, the ties are removed and a pattern remains on the strands. Thus, the final design of the ikat is created even before the piece is woven.

The true origin of ikat has not been determined. There is a possibility that the technique could have been developed by unrelated cultures in widely different areas at about the same time. The art of dyeing cloth and skin was already well-established some 3,000 years ago. Therefore, there is a possibility that more than one group of craftspeople could have discovered the idea of resist dyeing simultaneously. Undoubtedly, the commerce along the ancient trade routes served to help carry the technique from one area to another.

In Indonesia, fibers and bark cloth dating from 2,000 B.C. have been found, confirming that fabric making was known to the people. It is believed that along with other customs and practices the Chinese (Dong-Son) invasion, between 800 and 200 B.C., brought warp ikat to Indonesia. This process is still used to produce decorated cloth. Later, around the second century, weft ikat and many new pattern motifs were brought into the country from India.

Although textiles are now manufactured on machinery in most parts of the world, many weavers in Indonesia continue to produce ikat weaving by hand. Their production of cloth with its traditional symbols of wealth, fertility and the deities still carries personal meaning for both the weavers and the consumers. Made for weddings, ceremonies, burial cloths, sarongs and other garments, the ikat designs of today still match those of their ancestors of nearly 2,000 years ago.

SOCIAL SCIENCE EXPERIENCE

Concepts:

The use of traditional craftmaking methods may persist despite their obsolescence, because they embody meaning and perpetuate traditional values in changing cultures.

Utilitarian objects can spread the myths, stories, and values of a culture.

Objectives:

To consider the rationale for the persistence of tradition as embodied in contemporary craft production (in Indonesia and elsewhere).

To discover comparable examples of the existence of modern versions of traditional craft forms in our own (or other) culture(s).

To stimulate the discussion of the values (traditional or otherwise) embodied in craft objects.

Activities:

View as many examples (real or pictured) of ikat fabric renderings as possible.

Research the traditional symbols that appear on Indonesian ikats (figures in boats, turtles birds, floral design, and others). Find examples (real or pictures) of fabrics showing some of the symbols (animal, sun, and others) that have popular meaning in our own culture.

Discuss the meaning of the term, "cottage industry." Discover its significance in relation to the production of ikat cloth in Indonesia.

ART EXPERIENCE

Concepts:

Pre-planning can yield control and produce desired results.

Repeated and/or regular color transitions can yield unity.

Objectives:

To learn to warp a frame loom and to do a "tabby" weave.

To weave an ikat-style wall hanging with pre-dyed variegated yarn. Observe the pattern that emerges. Notice that the design gains unity through the repetition of colors and soft transition of edges.

Activity:

Materials: Wooden boards (1" x 2" thick) to make 12" x 24" frame looms (one for each student), 1" finishing nails, a hammer, knitting bobbins (or slats) for shuttles, variegated yarn with at least five colors that repeat at regular intervals, combs.

Directions: Assemble a frame loom. Then, measure and mark 40 evenly spaced intervals across its top and bottom. (Stagger their placement to prevent overlap or checking.) Drive in nails at the marks. Tie yarn to a top corner nail. Warp down and around the bottom corner nail and continue up and down across the loom until all of the nails are strung. Tie off. The warp should be taut. Wrap 6' of weft yarn around a shuttle and weave the first row, passing the shuttle over and under each warp in turn. Weave the second row in the opposite direction, passing under the warp strands that were passed over in the first row. Use the comb to press the weft rows tighter together. After a few rows of weaving, a pattern should emerge.

Leave the finished weaving on its frame for use as a wall decoration or cut and tie the warp strands, two by two, for a fringe.

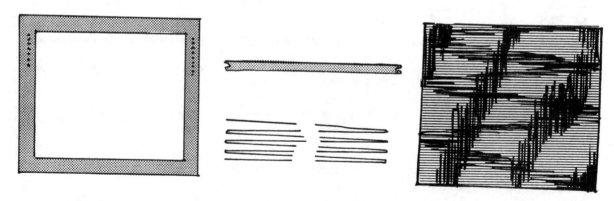

14. FARRAPEIRAS FROM SPAIN (A)

The labors of many people are required to make a piece of woolen cloth. Shepherds must watch over the sheep, the source of the woolen fibers. Then, the sheep must be shorn and their fleece, washed, dried, carded and spun into yarn which, finally, is woven into woolen fabric.

In Spain where weaving still is done in many homes, no blanket or piece of cloth is thrown away, simply because it is worn or torn. Instead, it is cut into strips about two or three inches wide. Then, the strips may be dyed and are pieced together, to be rewoven into a loose heavy cloth, called a "farrapeira," which is commonly used in Spain as a floor mat or furniture covering or an all-purpose sack for gathering and wrapping sundry items.

Spanish homemakers also use other fabrics, such as cotton, to weave lightweight ferrapeiras for use as aprons or cleaning cloths. Like patchwork quilts and braided rugs, Spanish farrapeiras are an effective way to recycle slightly damaged but still usable materials.

SOCIAL SCIENCE EXPERIENCE

Concept:

Conservation and recycling are practiced when products are scarce, costly, or labor-intensive.

Objectives:

To define the economic features and benefits of recycling.

Activities:

Assume the role of conservator and list the recyclable resources which are available to the classroom (newspapers, milk cartons, boxes). Identify possible recycling uses for them (woven mats, flower pots, cubby holes).

Research the recycling uses of garbage. Cite the cost advantages/limitations. Cite the dangers.

Read about artists and craftspeople who make things out of "junk."

Attend a craft fair. Speak with the craftspeople who use recycled materials in their products.

ART EXPERIENCE

Concept:

In weaving, designs develop from the repetition of value or color sequences.

Objectives:

To weave a mat of recycled fabric strips.

To introduce warping and weaving and practice sewing skills.

To create a repeating plaid or checkerboard pattern using two or more colors.

Activity:

Materials: Worn or discarded fabrics (curtains, drapes, towels, blue jeans, rags), scissors, sewing needles, thread, staples, a wooden frame (approximately 1 1/2' x 2'), an iron.

Directions: Separate fabrics into similar weights. Cut heavy or non-ravelling fabrics into 2" strips. Cut light fabrics (and ravelers) into 4"-wide strips. Fold their left edges inward to their centers and fold their right edges inward to their centers. Iron both folds (to crease them in place). Make warp strips as long as possible, at least 4" longer than the length of the frame, or loom. Select strips of colors to make checks or plaid. Staple warp strips to the outside edges of the wooden loom. Weave shorter, weft strips across the warps, pushing them together to make the fabric solid. When the mat is woven, finish by sewing all of the loose ends of the warp and the weft to the back of the mat.

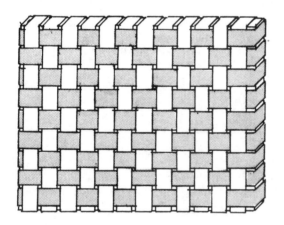
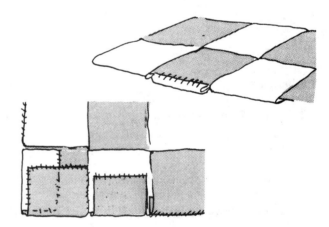

15. BAMBOO BASKETS OF THE MRUS (B)

The Mru culture of the uplands of southern Bangladesh is based on agriculture. Bamboo which grows in the region is one of the Mru's major resources. From bamboo, they make their houses, weapons for hunting and warfare, hats, toys, brooms, musical instruments, a form of paper and containers to hold their possessions.

The Mrus use split bamboo to make baskets. Sturdy, supple splits are tied together and fanned to form the spokes of a circle, around which thinner splits of bamboo are woven. The woven splits surrounding the hub of the spokes forms the bottom of the basket. When the weaving reaches the desired circumference, the warp splits are folded straight up, at right angles to the bottom, to form the basket's sides. Then, the weaving continues until the basket's sides reach the desired height. Then, the ends of the warp spokes are twisted back around the edge of the basket, and tucked end first into the twist. Mru baskets are woven with moist, freshly cut or water-soaked bamboo, which when dry hardens into a permanent shape.

SOCIAL SCIENCE EXPERIENCE

Concept:

Cultures create crafts with whatever materials are at hand. Where a single resource is abundant, some cultures have built an entire economy and lifestyle around it.

Objectives:

To identify the factors which link the economy of a culture to the natural resources in its environment.

To cite some cultures in which the relationship between a single resource and the culture's livelihood is the dominant factor in the culture's existence.

To compare the simple economy of the single resource economy with the complex economy of a culture such as our own; to recognize the way in which the growth of technology and expansion of trade affects a culture.

Activities:

Choose a single resource or material—cardboard, oak trees, aluminum foil, cows—design a fantasy society based on its use. Consider items such as clothing, shelter, food, and others. Also, specify the weather, environment and other factors which will influence the nature of the fantasy world.

Write a story or play exploring the experiences of an alien who comes from a simple culture into a complex one. Include examples of the alien's misunderstanding of the complex culture and examples of the misunderstanding of the alien, on the part of the inhabitants of the complex culture.

ART EXPERIENCE

Concept:

Form occupies and may enclose space.

Objectives:

To learn to weave a basket.

To demonstrate that the basket's form encloses space.

To suggest other examples of form enclosing space (such as hats, lampshades, vessels, tents).

To enhance skills in cutting, knotting and weaving.

To use the repetition of two colors to create a woven pattern.

Activity:

Material: Oak tag, colored paper, staples, scissors, string.

Directions: Cut colored paper strips, 30" long by 1/2" wide. Cut nine oak tag strips, 2' long by 1/2" wide, for the warps. Fold the nine strips in half. At the halfway mark, notch each strip, leaving a 1/4" space. Tie eight of the nine strips together with string at their notches and fan the strips out like 16 spokes of a wheel. Cut the ninth strip in half and insert one of the halves into the hub of the wheel (to make a 17th spoke, an odd number). To weave the basket bottom, start winding the string over and under the spokes, keeping each succeeding string circle as close as possible to the hub, until the circular weaving measures 6" across. Next, bend the warp spokes straight up at right angles to the circular base. Split one of the warps lengthwise (to make 18 spokes, an even number). Start with a 1/2" colored weft strip and weave it, under and over, all around the warp spokes. At the beginning, overlap the two weft ends, cut away any excess and staple the ends together. Alternate over and under and continue rows until the basket is 6" high. To end, weave the warps back down over the lip of the basket, folding half into the front of the basket and half into its back.

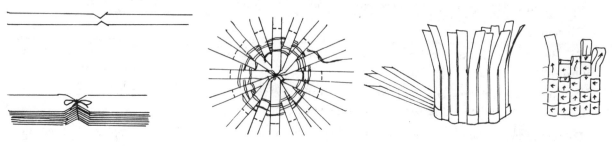

16. PERUVIAN SHAPE WEAVING (B)

Among the Inca Indians of ancient Peru, skilled craftspeople provided many of the necessities for daily living. Making good use of available materials, weavers transformed: the tough fibers of the maguey plant into linenlike cloth; cotton fibers from the lowlands into lightweight cloth; and the fleece of llamas, alpacas, huanacos and vicuna into warm cloth suitable for cold climates.

The fleece of the vicuna was so fine that it was reserved exclusively for the use of the nobility. Only the strictly-cloistered "Virgins of the Sun" were permitted to weave the lustrous vicuna fleece, into robes for members of the ruling class or into wall hangings for the Inca Temples. Since the days of the Spanish conquest, Europeans have admired vicuna fabric for its beautiful texture. Today, it is one of the world's most durable and expensive yarns.

One of the innovations of the ancient Peruvian weavers was the weaving of garments shaped to fit the individual. The method had many advantages: With no pieces to cut, there was no waste; all of the garment's edges were "finished" in the weaving process, with no need for hemming; all texture and design elements could be accurately placed; the weaving method was simple; and the loom could be easily rewarped and made ready to weave duplicate garments.

To create a garment with a definite shape, nails or pins were positioned close together along the outline of the garment to be woven. Then, a warp strand was strung, vertically, up and down, up and down, between the pins, as continuously as possible, until all of the pins at the top and the bottom were linked together. Next, the weft was woven, horizontally, over and under the warp strands, back and forth, as many times as necessary, to fill up the outline of the garment. As the weaving progressed, certain warp strands would become filled with weft strands and would be discontinued.

Special decorative designs could be woven into any garment or the designs could be woven first and, then, garments could be fashioned around them. As a variation, the shaping of circular garments would begin at their centers and pins (and warps to connect them) could be added as needed to complete the construction of the garment. Peruvian weavers used these methods to produce ponchos, skirts, shirts, vests, hats, bags and belts.

SOCIAL SCIENCE EXPERIENCE

Concepts:

The value of art and craft objects is determined by many criteria, including the base worth of the materials used; the amount of time, skill and labor involved in the creation; the rarity of the objects; their aesthetic qualities, and more.

Wearable wealth, such as jewelry, furs, and designer labels, symbolizes status in our own culture as well as in others.

Objective:

To identify and consider the reasons why garments woven from certain animal fibers assumed such importance in the Inca culture.

Activities:

Discuss the comparative values of various fabrics and the qualities that determine those values: texture, strength, warmth, durability;, flexibility, absorbency, ability to hold dye, porosity, "breathability" and others.

Discuss the uses of fabrics: canvas for sails, wool for sweaters, cotton terry for towels, nylon mesh for mosquito netting, and more.

Discuss the relation of fabrics to climate and lifestyle functionability.

List ten fabrics in order of their value, from cashmere, silk and satin to denim, nylon, and so forth.

Visit a fabric store and a yarn shop and feel samples of the various fabrics. Find out the prices of fabrics by the yard or ounce. Consider the reasons for these prices. Find out how the differences in "grades" of fabrics is achieved.

Design a "dream outfit" and explain your preference for certain fabrics.

ART EXPERIENCE

Concept:

Texture in a fabric is produced by combining a particular type of fiber with a particular type of weave.

Objectives:

To make a vest fitted to the individual student.

To experiment with texture by using different weights of yarns within one piece.

To emphasize symmetry by matching areas of texture in the front of a garment with equivalent areas on the back of garment.

Activity:

Materials: Plywood 2' x 5', 1 1/2" finishing nails, a hammer, a ruler, a shuttle, a yarn needle, yarns of different textures, a fabric marker, a tape measure.

Directions: Measure the student from the shoulder down (for the length of the vest). Measure across the back and shoulders (for the width of the vest). Draw an outline of the vest on the plywood, leaving a slit opening in the front and an oval opening at the top (for the neck). Hammer the nails 1/4" apart all the way around the garment outline. Begin the warping by tieing the end of a length of strong yarn onto a nail (at the lower corner, left or right). Then, warp the yarn up and down until the garment's outlined area is completely warped. Next, use yarns of different colors and textures to weave the area of vest. Be sure to match the front and the back areas. Pass the weft threads around the side nails to maintain width and shape.   At the shoulders, when the shuttle can no longer be passed through the warps, change to the yarn needle to weave the last rows. Remove the garment from the loom and sew it together under the arms. Add a fastener of string or buttons in the front.

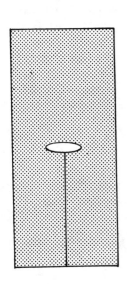
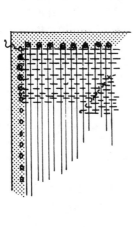
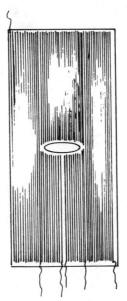
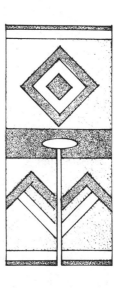

17. CHILKAT TWINING (B)

The Tlingit peoples, fourteen related tribes of the Pacific Northwest, have lived for a long time on the coast of southeastern Alaska and its nearby islands. One tribe, the Chilkat, has long been noted for its crafting of a special kind of decorative twined blanket. At one time Chilkat blankets were so highly favored for ceremonial wear by the other Tlingit chiefs that blankets became a basic unit of trade among the tribes.

Originally, Chilkat blankets were twined from mountain goat hair spun with shredded cedar bark. The twiners made their dyes from copper, hemlock and lichen. Their bold, stylized designs were also derived from elements in nature. To judge the proportions and amounts of materials that would be needed, twiners first painted their design patterns on boards that were the size of their finished blankets. Because the designs were usually symmetrical, the twiners only needed to paint one half of the design.

Twining produces a remarkably stable cloth and does not require a loom. Instead, the basic warp materials for a blanket are hung from a stable branch or rod and worked from the top down. Unlike weaving, twining works two horizontal weft strands at a time. At the first warp, Strand A passes over, while Strand B passes under. At the second warp, B passes over and A passes under. The weft strands continue alternating over and under each remaining warp, in turn. When completed, the warp threads at the top and bottom of the finished blanket are left untwined as fringe.

SOCIAL SCIENCE EXPERIENCE

Concepts:

The value of art and craft objects is determined by many criteria, such as: rarity; the amount of time, number of people and levels of skill required to produce the piece; aesthetic quality, usefulness, and more.

Wearable wealth, such as jewelry, furs, and designer labels, symbolizes status in other cultures as well as our own.

Objectives:

To observe and identify the value standards that exist in a culture.

To compare and contrast the value standards in one's own with those in other cultures.

Activities:

Visit an exhibit or consult visual reference materials depicting Northwest Indian cultural artifacts, especially blankets, totems, baskets, masks and others.

Determine the resources used in their production. Compare the Northwest resources with the types of resources used by other Indian groups, such as the Navaho and/or the Seminole tribes.

Find books, magazine articles about (and real examples of) contemporary Indian crafts. Compare the quality of artifacts made in the past for use by the Indians themselves with objects produced for the tourist trade.

ART EXPERIENCE

Concept:

Color contrast and simplicity of shape and line produce a striking design.

Objectives:

To weave a wall hanging.

To introduce twining technique and weighted warps.

To simplify a design into basic shapes and colors.

To use dynamic lines in making the design.

Activity:

Materials: Yarn in 6 colors, jute (between 200' to 280'), a 1" x 34" dowel, several feet of cord, scissors, a crochet hook, weights.

Directions: Draw a design in six colors (or less), using slanted lines to suggest movement. Next, tie cord at each end of the dowel and hang it horizontally in a secure place. Tie 50 (to 70) four-foot jute warps to the dowel. Tie weights to the bottom ends of the warps (in groups of 3 or 4). Allow the weights to hang free.

Beginning at the top, near the dowel, use a strand of yarn about 6' long to twine three rows of plain twining. (This is a heading, not the start of the design.) Find the center of the 6' strand and fold it (at that point) around the first warp strand. Then cross one 3' length under and the other 3' length over Warp 2. Proceed to Warp 3 and twine under and over again. Repeat all across the warps. Turn and twine back and turn again (until three rows are complete).

Next, choose a 6' strand of yarn in a color (according to the design) and start twining, as above. Add in or subtract colors (to copy design elements). Continue until the design is complete. For a finished look along the edges, wrap the two yarn strands around each other.

When all twining is complete, trim the warps top and bottom for a fringed effect.

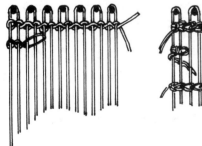  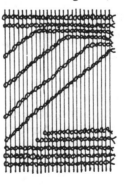 

18. WEAVERS OF SENEGAL (C)

In Senegal, there is one kind of loom for male weavers and another kind for female weavers. Since the 1500's, when the men's looms were first developed, they have remained almost unchanged. The narrow strips of cotton cloth produced by the men's looms are much admired by the Senegalese who prefer the colors and quality of the narrow fabric to that of the wider, coarser fabric pieces that are produced on the women's looms. The narrow strips are preferred because they have a special body and drape well. Also, fabrics of the most striking patterns can be created by sewing the narrower strips together with their stripes offset. The cotton strips can be made into cloaks, blankets, and sometimes even tents. In Senegal, cloth made on men's looms is part of the traditional "bride price" which is paid to the bride's father by the family of her husband-to-be.

While weaving, Senegalese men often sit together in a row, in the shade of a rough shelter or tree, as they work their four to six inch wide strips into lengths as long as 40 feet. The warps on each loom are weighted with a large stone which the weaver gradually draws towards himself, as the work progresses. A horizontal frame above each weaver's head supports two heddles, each fastened to pulleys which the weaver works with his feet, leaving his hands free to work the batten.

SOCIAL SCIENCE EXPERIENCE

Concept:

In some cultures traditions dictate different forms of behavior for men and for women.

Objectives:

To identify sex-related differences in cultural roles.

To determine the original, historic causes for the differences; the present causes for the perpetuation of the differences.

To determine the results of the differentiation on the people of the culture, in terms of their sense of authority, responsibility and worth, as well as their relative capabilities, and the compensation they receive.

Activities:

Discuss instances of the traditional separation of craft forms for men and women within a given culture. (Examples: Native American preparation of leather/hides, pottery making and the division in the use of geometric and natural designs.)

Work in a group and experience the feeling of social cohesion which results from all doing the same task, such as making a mural, a float or a mosaic.

Discuss the art concept and tell how it can be applied to other arts: music, architecture, dance, and others.

Examine pictures of African weaving and differentiate fabric produced by cloth and strip looms.

ART EXPERIENCE

Concept:

Make minor changes to add variety and visual interest to a fabric pattern.

Objectives:

To weave a cloth strip (perhaps belt length).

To create a repeating pattern with minor variations on a loom.

To practice warping and weaving.

Activity:

Materials: A loom, 2 heddles, a shuttle, 4 oz. to 6 oz. of yarn, a heavy rock or weight.

Directions: Set up (or make) a loom. (Its complexity will depend on the abilities of the weaver who will use it.) Warp the loom with 32 warp strands. Set up two heddles by tying 16 heddle strands to each heddle and numbering one heddle odd numbers (#1,3,5,7,9,11,13 through #31) and one heddle even numbers (#2,4,6,8,10,12 through 32). Warped strands are passed through the eye in the center of each heddle strand. Use cord to tie the heddles to a pulley (for ease in switching back and forth while weaving). Wind the weft yarn onto the shuttle and pass it through the shed created by lifting the odd-numbered heddle. Then, return the shuttle, from the opposite direction, by passing it through the shed created by lifting the even-numbered heddle. Continue alternating heddles for the length of the weaving.

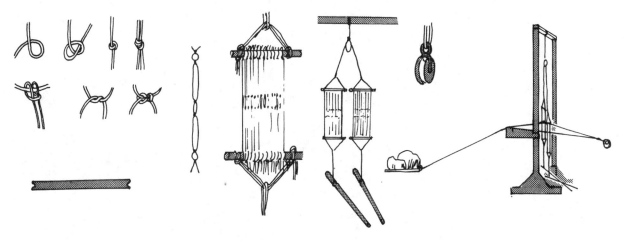

3

FIBERS AND FEATHERS

19. FEATHER NECKLACES OF BRAZIL (A)

Much of Brazil, the largest country in South America, is a part of the enormous Amazon River basin and is covered with rain forests. In contrast, however, Brazil's southeastern region is a dry, interior tableland. Artifacts and other signs of human habitation found there date back to Neolithic times.

In more recent times, many rich traditions have been developed by Brazil's vast and complex native Indian population. They like decoration. Even their everyday objects are considered unfinished until decorated. With many Brazilian tribes, forms of body decoration are especially important. For example, they create fanciful hair styles and paint their bodies and heads. More unusual, yet equally popular, is "shumperia," a type of ornamentation made of feathers and practiced by skilled Indian artists.

Today feather artists are considered among the most unique craftsmen of South America. Using the natural colors of feathers from up to forty different birds, the feather artists create authentic miniature versions of the precious, full-scale feather costumes that are worn in their tribal rites. The colors of the feathers they use have been assigned symbolic meanings. White represents goodness and energy, whereas black symbolizes negative feelings, and red stands for health and the earth.

SOCIAL SCIENCE EXPERIENCE

Concept:

Cultures develop symbolic languages.

Objectives:

To recognize specific examples of the symbolic color language in contemporary North American culture.

To trace the origins of the meanings attached to the color symbols.

Activities:

Discuss the color symbols of religious rituals and national holidays.

List color symbols which derive their meaning from nature: red/blood.

Discuss the emotional meanings of colors: (wedding) white, (funeral) black, (emergency equipment) red.

Research the relationship between color variations and people's psychological reactions to them: red/hot, green/serene, blue/cool.

Select your favorite personal colors and use them to design (and make) a personal flag. Write an essay explaining the meaning of these colors in regard to your background, your personality, your feelings.

ART EXPERIENCE

Concept:

Contrasts in color or texture add variety, visual interest and emphasis.

Objectives:

To make a necklace of beads and feathers.

To choose colors with symbolic meanings.

To show the contrast between bead and feather textures.

To control emphasis through choice of color.

To develop skills in creating symmetrical balance, threading, tying, wrapping and knotting.

Activity:

Materials: One yard of heavy macrame' cord, bright yarns, colored feathers, beads to string on macrame' cord, beads with holes large enough to fit over quill ends of feathers.

Directions: Cut the yarn into 9" lengths. Thread beads onto the macrame' cord. Knot the yarn pieces between the larger beads on the cord, as shown. Thread two smaller beads onto each end of the yarn. Apply glue to the quill ends and secure with beads and a separate short piece of yarn, as shown. Knot the ends of the macrame' cord and tie the finished necklace around neck.

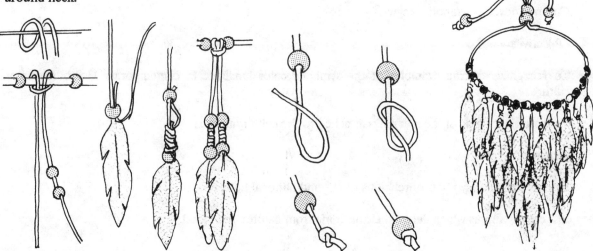

20. WOVEN HOUSE FRONTS OF TORADJA (A)

The Toradja people live on Celebes, also called Sulawesi, a mountainous island about half way between Australia and mainland Asia. Tana Toradja (the land of the Toradja) is located on the western branch of the island on a mountainside. The people have very little money and work primarily as farmers, raising livestock, rice, cassava and other vegetables.

Toradja houses are unique. Most striking are the bamboo roofs that sweep upward at each end to peaks of forty or fifty feet. Pointed, like the bow and stern of a boat, the roof peaks look remarkably like the canoes that originally brought the Toradja people to the island. The high peaks are supported by bamboo poles, while the remainder of the house is braced by living tree trunks. The exterior walls of a Toradja house are made of decorative woven bamboo panels, interrupted at intervals with open windows and balconies. The panels are made of thin painted planks woven in endless variations of a checkerboard pattern, achieved by skipping over or under two or more planks.

SOCIAL SCIENCE EXPERIENCE

Concepts:

Cultures often design architecture in imitation of a familiar natural or manmade environment, such as a cave, mountains or a ship.

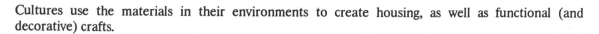

Cultures use the materials in their environments to create housing, as well as functional (and decorative) crafts.

Objectives:

To note and list examples of architecture derived from imitating environmental sources.

To note and list examples of architecture designed to capitalize on the advantages of its environment; to withstand the disadvantages of its environment.

Activities:

Discuss the influence of available materials on the construction of buildings; explore considerations of size, durability, utility, and others (the requirements for a fortress? a desert dwelling? a house in a flood zone? a moon habitat?)

Discuss the historic development of architectural styles in your community and in the nation as a whole. What kinds of houses did immigrants from other countries build? How was their construction altered by the availability of materials?   by considerations of their new environment?

Choose a feature in the local environment (real or imaginary: a mountain, a volcano, a ship) and design a building to imitate it. Indicate the construction materials needed to imitate it.

Choose an animal habitat: a bird's nest, anthill, beaver dam.   Design a room or a building that incorporates the design features of the animal habitat.

ART EXPERIENCE

Concepts:

High contrast between geometric designs provides a rhythmic pattern.

Repetition of shape and color create a unified pattern.

Objectives:

To develop a high contrast design in black and white for two-color weaving.

To emphasize the design with a central motif.

To practice making rhythmic design patterns.

To foster skill in cutting and weaving.

Activity:

Materials: 1 Black and 1 white sheet of construction paper (12" x 18"), scissors, a stapler, paste.

Directions: Cut black paper into strips, 18" long x 1/2" wide. Fold the white paper lengthwise in half and mark along the fold at 1/2" intervals. Mark corresponding 1/2" intervals along the outer edges and cut slits from the fold to within 1/2" of the outer edges. (For diagonal slits, mark a 1/2" border around the paper; bend the sheet up from one corner to make a 45° angle; mark every 1/2" on the fold. Draw from the corner to the center mark and draw lines parallel to this line from one outside border to the other outside border. Cut slits on the lines through the fold.) Unfold the white paper. Begin weaving the black strips through the slits at the center of the white paper. Make a design for the center motif. Then fill in both sides. Paste or staple the ends when finished.

21. YARN PAINTING OF THE HUICHOLS (A)

The Huichol Indians of Mexico are descendants of the ancient Aztecs who enjoyed a powerful and sophisticated culture until the Spaniard Hernando Cortez and his conquistadors took power in Mexico in the sixteenth century.   Today, the Huichols make the most of what they have by farming their mountainous territory to earn a meager living.   Because the forage on their ranches is too sparse to support cattle, the Huichol raise sheep for wool.

Huichol craftspeople use brightly-colored yarns for wrappings, tyings, weaving and yarn painting. They make their colors with homemade vegetable dyes, and sometimes supplement their materials with commercially-dyed yarns.

A yarn painting is made by spreading warm beeswax on a smooth wooden surface. Lengths of yarn are then pressed into place. Shapes are outlined, then filled with patterns and whirls. The entire area of the painting is covered with yarn figures of people, animals, plants, insects, the sun, moon or stars. As the wax cools, it hardens, fixing the yarn in place, with no discoloration.

SOCIAL SCIENCE EXPERIENCE

Concept:

Cultures create crafts with whatever materials are at hand.

Objectives:

To identify the factors which cause resources to dwindle.   To identify the consequences of that loss.

To identify the benefits that must occur in order for cultures to supplement or replace original products and materials with imported ones.

Activities:

Examine the role of petroleum products in the world today.   Consider the consequences if the petroleum supply should run out.   What alternatives might be developed to take petroleum's place?

Design a picture or a sculpture of a functional object.   (Think of Andy Warhol's tomato soup can.)   Make the picture or sculpture as realistic as possible.   Think of 10 points of comparison that could be made between the real and fake versions (color, texture, size, scarcity and others).

ART EXPERIENCE

Concept:

Shapes are areas of color, texture or value.

Objectives:

To make a yarn painting.

To simplify a representational scene or single figure into basic shapes.

To use color and contour to define shapes by contrasting them with the background.

To develop skill in drawing and gluing.

Activity:

Materials: A small square of plywood, large and small pots, beeswax, a hot plate or candle warmer, a table knife, scissors, a stick, newspapers, yarns of many colors.

Directions: Draw a design on the plywood square.   Place the square on some newspaper. Warm the beeswax in a pan set in a larger pan of water.   Spread the warm wax very thinly on a single shape of the design.   Outline the shape with yarn, then fill in the yarn design details, and continue to use the yarn to fill in the other areas of the design.   Press the yarns into the wax with a stick.   Areas of the same color and value may be set off from each other with black or white outlines.   Finally, use at least four strands of yarn to make a border around the edge of the wooden square. Keep the strands close together.

22. ASMAT RAINCOATS (A)

New Guinea, one of the largest island countries in the world, is a land of tall mountains, dense jungles, and near-primitive tribes. The Asmats, a rugged people, inhabit the low marshes of the southwest. Their environment is hostile, bounded by an irregular coastline and subjected periodically to heavy rainfalls that drench the land and swell the rivers.

The themes of Asmat art center around death, masculine prowess, war and the spirits of nature. Much Asmat art is designed to make the warriors appear fierce to their foes. The Asmats occupy themselves with self-adornment, such as face-painting and the making of traditional costumes, decorated with beads, teeth and skulls.

Other Asmat tribal crafts are more practical. The women weave mats and, with rains so frequent, have developed an Asmat "raincoat," a unique tent-like covering. The raincoat is made from pandanus leaves that are tied together and overlapped like a thatched roof. The natural grooves in the leaves help to channel the rainwater to the ground, away from the wearer. In New Guinea, the materials for the raincoat, like the rain, are always close at hand.

SOCIAL SCIENCE EXPERIENCE

Concept:

Societies with few resources make extensive use of the resources that are available.

Objective:

To identify the ways in which people creatively solve problems and make improvements in their lives.

Activities:

Discuss how cultures use the natural properties of local materials to benefit themselves. (Example: Asmat tribespeople noted the water-repellant properties of pandanus leaves.)

List ten outstanding examples of the clever use of available resources. Include references to contemporary, local, national, foreign, stone age and, even, imaginary cultures (as in films or books).

Invent a new use for a natural material from your own neighborhood.

Debate the concepts: "Form follows function" vs. "Form determines function."

ART EXPERIENCE

Concept:

Ordered repetition creates unity of design.

Objective:

To make a double-layered "raincoat" in which the alternation of strips protects the seams of the inner layer.

Activity:

Materials: Heavy wrapping paper (3' long), scissors, staples, masking tape.

Directions: Cut 27 to 31 strips of paper 4" wide and 3' long. Lay 13, 15, or 17 strips on a working surface, parallel and just touching each other. Cover the strips with a second layer of strips, staggered to overlap the seams of the strips in the underlayer. Make the edges at the tops of all the strips even and staple each top strip twice (once to each of the two under-strips that it partly covers.) Repeat across the bottom edge. Fold the stapled strips in half at their midpoint, to form the back of the coat. Leave an opening for the front of the coat, but staple the strips that form the "hood" several times. Also, tape the strips together.

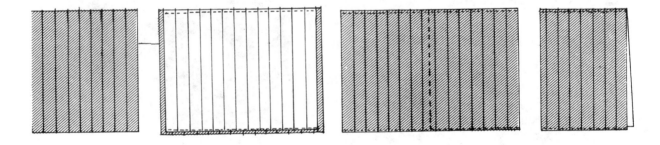

23. NATIVE AMERICAN QUILL WORK (A)

Quill work was a popular craft among many native American tribes across the North American continent. Although porcupine quills were scarce, or even unknown in many places in the west, a quill trade was developed between tribes in the east (the suppliers) and tribes in the west (the consumers), in order to supply the demands for materials. More recently, however, in most tribes quill work has been replaced by beadwork as a decorative and saleable craft. The availability of multi-colored, ready-made beads, for use instead of the rare and difficult to prepare quills, made the changeover not merely acceptable, but welcome.

In order to work with quills, they first had to be colored with natural dyes. Then they were softened in warm water, after which they were sewn like needles through small holes punched into birch bark or leather. The sewing process was simple: a small sharp instrument was used to pierce a hole in the bark; then, a quill was inserted from the back, pulled through to the front and pulled through another hole to the back of the piece. Each quill was carefully placed to form one part of a definite, usually geometric pattern, starting at the pattern center and working outward. The finished quill work was then dampened, stretched flat and dried. Later it would be used as decoration on a garment, moccasins or some other special item. Quill work was the forerunner of both bead and broom straw work which use many of the quill work patterns.

Among the Sioux in the American West, quill work was not assigned exclusively to either men or women, as were the other crafts. However, a division of the labor did exist. Women did the geometric designs and men did the designs used to represent real subjects.

SOCIAL SCIENCE EXPERIENCE

Concepts:

Role assignment by gender is a component of many cultures.

Artisans often employ a new, more efficient or less expensive technique or material to imitate a valued object.

Objectives:

To identify some gender-related role assignments in other cultures, and in one's own culture.

To identify the reasons why techniques and materials used to make craft items may be substituted over the course of time. To list examples of the phenomenon.

Activities:

Make a film, a drawing, a collection of new items or a poster graphically defining and depicting changes in gender-related roles.

Research to find out the reasons behind changes in gender-related roles. Consider: Rosey the Riveter; the first typists, stenographers, others.

ART EXPERIENCE

Concept:

Texture can reinforce the unity of shape in a design.

Objectives:

To make a "quill work" design with broom straws.

To use broom straws of the same shape, size or color to define shapes within the design.

To use different colors or densities to contrast the shapes.

To exercise cutting and gluing skills.

Activity:

Materials: A piece of heavy cardboard (5" x 7"), broom straws, white glue, food coloring, scissors.

Directions: Draw a geometric design on the cardboard. Dye some straws with food coloring. Keep others in their natural color. Brush a coat of 1/3 glue and 1/2 water over the cardboard design to seal it. Starting from the center of the design, precut straws to fit its shapes. Then, apply glue to the shapes and press on the precut straws, placing them close together. Continue until the entire surface of the design is covered.

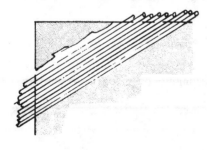  

24.   FEATHER ARMBANDS OF ARNHEM LAND (B)

In Arnhem Land the people give the stars and the sun aboriginal names and speak of them as if they were flesh and blood beings..."The Morning Star trails a feathered string behind herself, which ties her to her home." Thus do the fishermen and hunters of Arnhem Land, in northern Australia, explain the presence of Barnambir, the morning star, one of their deities.

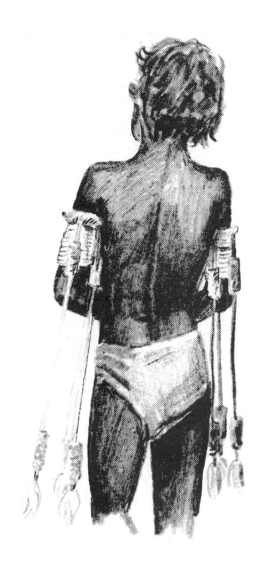

Historically, Arnhem Land has been influenced by New Guinea and Indonesia, resulting in a cultural variety which stresses the visual and links art and myth together. The people are themselves works of art, as they constantly strive to impress one another with the intricacy and beauty of the colors and designs that they wear. They practice face-painting and tattooing, and many of their traditions require that they adorn themselves with feathers, flowers and leaves. As a part of their coming of age ceremony, the youths of Arnhem wear feathered strings on their armbands to symbolize that as boys, they are, like the morning star before sunrise, still tied to their homes. However, after the ceremony, they are no longer boys and can no longer live at home. Instead, they must live in a bachelor camp until they marry.

SOCIAL SCIENCE EXPERIENCE

Concept:

The degree of freedom in personal expression varies from culture to culture. Less structured cultures often allow more individual aesthetic variety. More structured societies often possess more rigid standards of conformity.

Objectives:

To recognize and list examples of societies or cultures exhibiting obvious symbolic meanings in personal dress, choice of accessories or hairstyles.

To note the use of adornment to signify certain traits or status in societies or cultures. To explain the purpose and the practice of the behavior.

Activities:

Discuss the uniforms of various clubs, teams, and professions (Scouts, football team, police) and contrast them with "optional" uniforms of various social groups (jeans and T-shirts, gray business suits).

Contrast cultures in which standards of dress are rigid with those in which individual expression is valued.

Identify the symbols and insignia contemporary people wear: scout badges, police badges, school team logos (Tigers, Jets), religious medals, motorcycle gang "colors," rock stars on T-shirts, class rings and pins, and others.

Discuss the meaning of the expressions, "He/she wears a lot of hats," and "You can't judge a book by its cover." What can we tell about people from the way they dress?

Design (and make) a symbolic costume for an imaginary group or club. Include a hat, jacket and badge.

ART EXPERIENCE

Concept: Contrasting the textures of elements creates emphasis, variety and visual interest.

Objectives:

To make a feathered armband.

To select feathers to contrast with yarn and rope.

To foster skill in wrapping, tying and measuring.

Activity:

Materials: 8' of cotton or jute rope (1/4" in diameter), scissors, colored feathers, colored yarn, white glue.

Directions: Make tufts of feathers at each end of the rope by lightly gluing "skirts" of feathers around the rope ends. Also, wrap the skirts with yarn three (or more) times until they are secure. Move along the rope, to 1" away from each end, and create two more feather skirts as before. After the glue has dried, wrap the feather armband around the upper arm, as shown.

25. HANDMADE PAPERS OF FRANCE (B)

The French are justly famous for the crafting of fine quality handmade papers. But today only a few paper mills remain in existence in which the work of papermaking is done almost entirely by hand.

The production of paper requires the use of enormous amounts of water. For that reason, most paper mills are situated near large rivers.

Besides lots of water, the making of elegant paper also requires the recycling of a very inelegant material—cloth rags. First the rags are separated by color. Then, to make special kinds of paper, some are set aside for use as they are, but most are thoroughly bleached to a uniform whiteness. Next, the rags are shredded and mixed with water in enormous pulp vats, where they are beaten into a fibrous mass which is then thickened with starch, a binding agent. Then a framed screen dips into the pulp mixture and picks up a thin layer of pulp. The excess water is drained off and drying begins. Finally, the damp pulp passes through a series of rollers and driers until it is uniformly flat and dry. Varying the pressure and temperature of the rollers produces papers of different weights and textures.

SOCIAL SCIENCE EXPERIENCE

Concepts:

Conservation and recycling are practiced when products are scarce, costly or labor-intensive.

Conservation and recycling procedures can yield useful and aesthetically pleasing products.

Objectives:

To observe and analyze the paper manufacturing industry, especially noting the effects of electrical power and automated labor.

To identify the elements involved in a manufacturing process: materials, equipment, labor and so forth; to compare labor-intensive, unique products to mass-produced products, in terms of costs and quality.

Activities:

Gather data on various kinds of paper. Identify the materials used to make each kind.

Collect samples of high-to-low grade papers and make an exhibit of them.

Write to paper manufacturers for information.

Tour a paper mill.

Learn the history of paper-making.

Discuss the uses of paper, practical and decorative/aesthetic, in modern society.

ART EXPERIENCE

Concept:

Basic materials affect the texture of art works.

Objectives:

To make paper.

To learn the papermaking process.

To perfect techniques of shredding and mixing.

Activity:

Materials:　Paper, lint from a clothes dryer, a measuring cup, starch, a blender, a dish pan, 2 frames (same size, approximately 9" x 12"), wire screening (larger than the area of one of the frames), a stapler, construction paper, a stick (to support the frame while draining), a piece of blanket or felt (the same size as the frame, a steam iron, a bowl, gelatin, a brush.

Directions:　Staple the screening over one frame (pull it tight).　Tear the paper into small bits.　In the blender, macerate 2 cups of water, 1/4 cup of paper and 1/4 cup of lint, into a pulp.　Add two cups of starch.　Add more lint and paper, if needed to bring the mixture to a "milkshake" consistency.　Pour into a pan until deeper than the combined height of the frames. Place the screened frame, screen side up in the pan.　Place the second (unscreened) frame on top.　Tilt the pan back and forth until the screen is covered with pulp.　Lift the frames and let them drain over the pan, placing one edge on the pan's rim and the other edge on a stick (laid across the pan).　Prepare a thick gelatin in the bowl.　Pick up the two frames from their draining position and remove the top frame.　Turn the paper pulp layer off onto the blanket piece (or felt).　Brush gelatin on the top surface of the paper pulp layer and let it dry over-night.　When completely dry, iron the dry paper to smooth its surface.

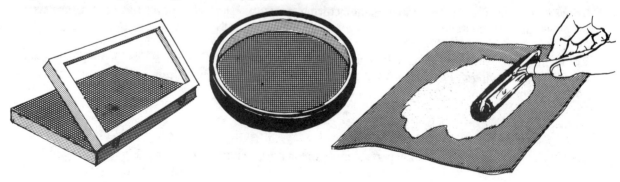

26. GOLDEN STRAWS OF MALAYSIA (B)

Malaysia is a small country situated at the crossroads between India, China, Indonesia and Australia. Thailand, its nearest neighbor to the north, connects Malaysia with the continent of Asia. A tropical country, Malaysia has both palm-fringed beaches and mountains that range from Penang in the north to the boundary with the independent republic of Singapore on the southern tip of the Malay peninsula.

Artists of Malaysia have developed art and craft forms that make use of materials made or grown in their own region. One of the most unique techniques uses straw to make realistic pictures. The artists place stalks of straw on a background of black or deep aqua fabric, creating exciting lines and textures by varying the direction, length, and density of the straw. Their subjects are inspired by the scenes and activities of their environment. Floral designs are common, influenced by Malaysia's lush jungle vegetation. Ships and the ocean are also popular, and as a result, fleets of straw junks, dhows and sampans constantly sail the seas of Malaysian art work.

SOCIAL SCIENCE EXPERIENCE

Concepts:

Cultures create crafts with whatever materials are at hand.

Products produced by regional craftspeople for trade do not necessarily represent their best creative abilities or their highest standards of workmanship.

Objectives:

To research the Malaysian economy and determine the reasons why the materials that are readily available in an environment are those chosen for use by native craftspeople.

To identify the reasons why souvenirs produced for trade are not necessarily representative of a culture's best craft work.

Activities:

Devise a marketing scheme for Malaysian straw pictures. Identify to whom they could be sold; figure what elements would be involved in the cost of straw pictures of various sizes; figure what the price would have to be for various sizes.

Hypothesis: Straw is no longer available in Malaysia. Figure out a substitute material with which Malaysian crafts people could work to produce their pictures. Experiment to see if the new material will work. Also, figure its cost relative to the straw. Will the new material work?

ART EXPERIENCE

Concept:

An aggregation of straight line elements can produce shape, texture and pattern.

Objectives:

To make a representational picture with straws.

To create shapes by varying the length of parallel straws.

To create contrasts in shape and texture by varying the direction of straws.

To create contrast in texture by varying the density of straws.

To develop planning and arranging skills.

Activity:

Materials: Natural straws, scissors, dark fabric, glue, heavy cardboard, white chalk.

Directions: Glue cloth to the cardboard. On a sheet of paper, draw a design the same size as the cardboard. To transfer the design, chalk the back of the design. Then, lay the paper, chalk-side down, on the cloth and trace (transfer) the design onto the paper. (Remove the paper and a chalk version of the design will be on the cloth.) Next, pre-cut straws to fit the design, using the original pattern as a guide. Select the heaviest straws for lines that stand alone. Glue the thinner straws side by side to fill in shapes; also, to create patterned areas, vary the direction of the straws. Apply glue to single straws if they are to be used as solitary lines or outlines. To fill in shapes or to create patterned areas, apply glue to the area, then lay in the straws.

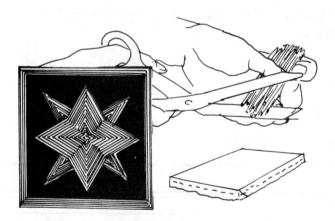

27. KOREAN FEATHER FANS (C)

Korea, long a buffer between its powerful neighbors, China and Japan, is now turning its energies toward self-improvement.   In addition to promoting industrialization and better living conditions, Korea's goals include the preservation of its own heritage.   Shrines and artifacts are protected, while the creation of new architecture and art forms are encouraged to conform to traditional high standards.   Koreans feel that material success must not be achieved at the expense of their own unique culture.

Visitors to Korea can find many opportunities to sample a taste of Korea's traditional art forms and foods.   One beautiful spectacle is a traditional dance in which women costumed in colorful silk robes and opulent headdresses carry large and equally colorful fans. Made of lacquered bamboo and rice paper, the fans are tipped with graceful feathers that catch the breeze as the dancers move.

SOCIAL SCIENCE EXPERIENCE

Concept:

Despite their obsolescence, traditional craft objects and customs often are protected and preserved, because they perpetuate traditional values and embody meaning for a changing culture.

Objectives:

To identify the values, both tangible and intangible, to be derived from the historical preservation of artifacts and architectural specimens.

Activities:

Research the governmental, educational, corporate, religious, and other organizations who support the preservation of the buildings, artifacts and institutions that are parts of the national heritage. Examine their reasons, from altruism to tax breaks, for doing so.

Examine actual case studies in which preservation is practiced; find some that result in the common good; find others which are counterproductive.

ART EXPERIENCE

Concept:

Contrast in color or texture can create a sense of movement in a design.

Objectives:

To make a feathered fan.

To use complementary colors to gain contrast between the textures of feathers and fan.

To emphasize the semi-circular shape with a design to fit the area.

To foster craftsmanship in cutting, tying and gluing.

Activity:

Materials: Feathers, tissue paper, wooden coffee stirrer sticks, paper clips, a drill with a 1/16" bit, paint, white glue, tape.

Directions: Paint the stirrer sticks to match the color of the feathers. Cut two semi-circles of tissue paper, each with a radius measuring the same as the length of the sticks. Cut a 3" semi-circle from the center of both tissue paper circles (to act as "windows" for the sticks to show through). Stack 6 to 8 sticks (and temporarily tape them together). Then, at one end of the pile of sticks, drill a hole through all of the sticks. Pass a paper clip through the holes (to fasten the sticks together). (Then, remove the temporary tape.) Glue feathers to the opposite ends of the sticks, leaving 1/2" of feather sticking up at each stick end. Lay the bundle of sticks on top of the tissue paper. Spread the sticks out evenly in a fan shape. Mark their positions on the paper. (That is where the glue will be placed.) Put glue on the stirrers and attach them to the tissue papers (at the marks), first glue the paper on the back, and then the paper on the front. Wrap the paper ends around the end sticks.

For a shiny finish, brush the paper with a mixture of half glue and half water. When dry, decorate and make desired creases.

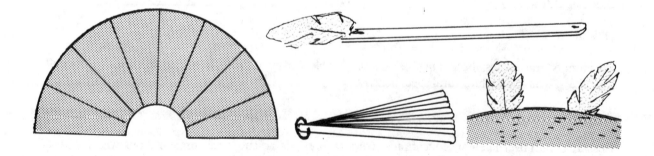

28. SEPIK SLEEPING MATS (C)

The Sepik River tribes live on New Guinea's southeastern coast at the mouth of the Sepik River, which serves as an intertribal trade route and provides a ready source of food.   The Sepiks are a primitive people, slow to relinquish their traditional ways.   Their skillfully made handcrafts, especially their decorated bowls, tools, spears and fierce masks are represented in museum collections around the world.

The Sepiks also make sleeping mats, baskets, wrappers, dividing screens, rugs and oil from the leaves of the sago palm, a primary forest resource.   Sago palm leaves or fronds are long and durable, and their oil makes them waterproof. The lengthwise fibers of the fronds give them great strength.   Their stems serve as finished edges that won't unravel.   The fibers on one half (or side) of a leaf are cut off in strips for use as weft material, while the fibers of the other half are also slit into strips but left attached to the stem, to form a sort of instant warp.   Using this basic material, the Sepik people fashion all kinds of useful woven items.

SOCIAL SCIENCE EXPERIENCE

Concept:

Societies with few resources make extensive use of whatever is available.   Some have built an entire economy and lifestyle around a single resource.

Objectives:

To identify some of the characteristics of a primitive culture.

To analyze the dependence on oil of a culture with an industrialized economy.   To hypothesize the consequences if the resource becomes unavailable.

Activities:

Discuss whether the intentional use of "primitive" materials and technology by a craftsperson can qualify a craft object as being primitive (even if the craftsperson is not a member of a primitive culture).   Also, if something is handmade from natural materials, is it necessarily primitive?

Plan a camping trip (for a day or for overnight). Make lists of the food and equipment needed for the trip. Place restrictions and requirements on the items to be selected, such as: the amount of weight and number of pieces to be carried, the amount of money to be spent, the necessity of a balanced diet, the need for liquid. Go on the trip.

Find pictures of Sepik arts and crafts, as well as the works of other primitive cultures. Compare them with items made by young children. Explain the differences between the two in terms of materials, functions, skill levels and others.

ART EXPERIENCE

Concept:

Repetition of shape and color create a unified pattern.

Objectives:

To make a plaited mat.

To develop pattern through repetition.

To learn plaiting, how to turn corners, and precision cutting.

Activity:

Materials: A 4' length of brown wrapping paper, paste, pins, scissors.

Directions: Cut the wrapping paper into sixteen 4' by 3/4" strips. Fold one strip in half lengthwise and pin it (at its fold) to a working surface. Then, at their centers, fold the remaining strips in half at 45 degree angles. Place each of the fifteen strips, one by one, at their folds, under the upper half of the pinned strip. Next, weave each of the strips over and under the others. The ends of strips which project beyond the last fold should be turned back at 45 degrees and inserted to form a finished outer edge for the mat.

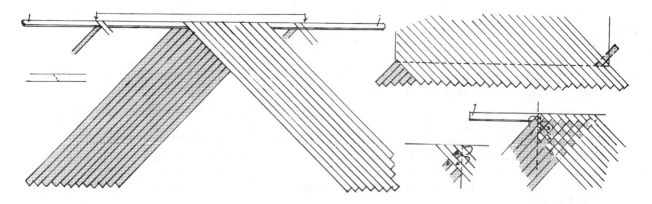

29. MAORI PLAITED HEADBANDS (C)

The ancestors of the Maori traveled to New Zealand from Tahiti and other Polynesian islands in canoe-like long boats. The Maori are proud of their heritage, and today they work together to reenact the arrival and original lifestyle of their ancestors. During these reenactments the Maori men wear loin cloths and plaited headbands just as their ancestors did in ancient battles.

The Maori are masters of many craft media. They value complex ornamentation as well as technical virtuosity in craftsmanship, and they continue to use traditional techniques, motifs and materials. The four-strand plaiting used to create a Maori headband must be executed with precision in order to produce a textured, perfectly hexagonal design. The vertical grain of the palm leaf from which the bands are woven serves to emphasize the hexagonal pattern. When the weaving is completed, the loose tip ends of the palm leaf are used to tie the headband at the back of the head.

SOCIAL SCIENCE EXPERIENCE

Concept:

The use of traditional craft objects may persist despite their obsolescence, because they perpetrate traditional values and embody a sense of permanence for a changing culture.

Objectives:

To note and analyze examples of historical reenactment, such as: the landing of the Pilgrims, the first Thanksgiving, significant battles and other famous firsts. To consider: What kinds of occasions call for pageantry? Why is it important for people to learn about and celebrate their own heritage?

To consider the reasons, aesthetic, symbolic and social, for people to develop a "typical" garment or other item.

Activities:

Study the "pageantry" (customs) of the ancestors of members of the class.

Locate New Zealand and Tahiti on a map. Study the Maori as an example of a tribal culture that has managed to maintain its identity in the modern world. Discuss how reenactment and traditional crafts have been essential enabling elements in this survival.

ART EXPERIENCE

Concept:

In weaving, designs develop from the repetition of value or color elements.

Objectives:

To plait a headband with a continuous design that is created by folding.

To use contrasting colors of paper to highlight the rhythmic progression of the pattern.

To learn to follow a pattern.

To gain skill in plaiting.

Activity:

Materials: Eight paper strips (24" long x 1 1/2" wide) in four colors, paper clips, paste.

Directions: Fold the strips lengthwise to a width of 3/4". Using four strips, follow the pattern in the diagram. To begin, secure the strips with paper clips. Fold two strips from the right, then two from the left. Proceed, making neat, tight folds, keeping the edges parallel with one another in a hexagonal pattern. Paste on replacement strips as needed to complete the headband. When the weaving is long enough to fit around the head in a circle, finish the headband by pasting and tucking in the loose ends of the strips.

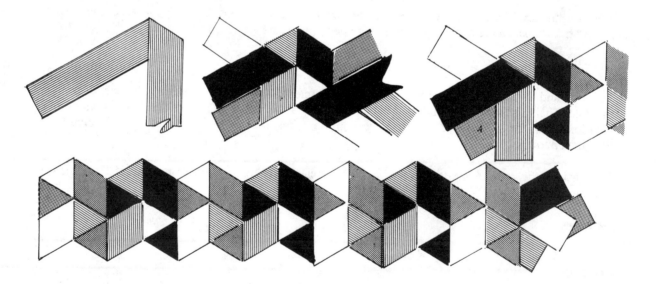

4

SHEETS, WIRES AND INGOTS

30. AMULETS OF LADAKH (A)

Nestled in the Himalayan mountains, Ladakh is one of the most remote districts of India. Formerly an independent monarchy on the caravan routes to Tibet, Chinese Turkestan and Kashmir, today Ladakh is overshadowed by its larger neighbors: Russia to the north, Pakistan to the west, and China to the east. Because the growing season in Ladakh is very short, trade and commerce have become more important in its economy than farming.

The population of Ladakh is approximately half Buddhist and half Moslem. Both groups share certain cultural practices. For example, Buddhist and Moslem children, alike, wear protective amulets to ward off evil spirits. The parents of Ladakh, like parents everywhere, hope for good fortune for their children. The amulets reflect the influence of Indian and Chinese art and often show a traditional symbol of luck or power, such as a dragon or a deity, surrounded by a curvilinear frame.

SOCIAL SCIENCE EXPERIENCE

Concept:

People in most cultures actively pursue the quest for good fortune, especially for their children.

Objectives:

To recognize and appreciate the values shared universally by people in cultures everywhere; to discover examples of extreme and unique values or beliefs held by individual cultures.

Activities:

Discuss symbols of luck in our own and other cultures. Collect samples of the objects which will give good (or bad) luck.

Design and conduct a survey among family members to discover good luck rituals and symbols that they believe in or know about. Try to find some unusual examples and trace their origins.

ART EXPERIENCE

Concept:

Outlining and framing add unity to an image.

Objectives:

To make a good luck amulet with a framed symbol of luck.

To incise a design and gain skill in casting a simple open mold.

To learn to carve in reverse.

Activity:

Materials: "Sculpt metal" or self-hardening clay, silver spray paint, plaster, a bucket, plastic bowls (butter type), a scraper, a pin back.

Directions: Mix plaster with water to achieve a heavy cream consistency.   Fill bowls half full, tap them firmly, to remove bubbles, and let the mixture set until it dries.   (Do not pour waste plaster into sink or toilet drains; let it harden, then throw it away.)   Design an amulet. Carve its shape into the plaster, 1/8" deep.   Smoothly carve out the design's details.   Do not "undercut" (make overhanging cliffs in the plaster) or the undercut plaster will "grip" the sculpt metal (or clay) and prevent it from being removed from the mold.

To form the amulet, press the sculpt metal (or clay) into the carved design and let it harden. When hard, the metal (or clay) should be loosened with a blade and pried out of the plaster with care to not injure the molded amulet.   Next, spray paint the amulet with a metallic color. Then, use glue to attach a pin to its back.

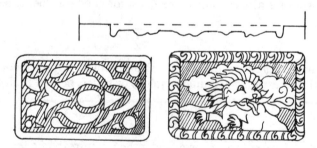

31. A LINK WITH THE NEW WORLD (A)

Although the riches of the New World supplied new wealth to the royal treasuries of Europe, much of the booty was lost to shipwreck.   Sixteenth century ships were not always seaworthy, and many a cargo of gold, merchandise and precious gems found a watery home at the bottom of the sea as ships sank in violent storms or foundered on treacherous reefs.

Recently, modern methods of search and recovery have yielded numbers of treasure troves from sunken trade ships, including trade goods, religious artifacts, and the personal possessions of the passengers and crews.   These newfound treasures have added much to our present day knowledge of the colonial activities in the Americas.

Among the bullion, ingots, goblets and ancient coins found in a recently discovered Spanish wreck, divers found gold forged into chains with unsoldered links. The chains were worn by travelers who could pry open a link and have it weighed and valued for use in place of money. The chains were the original instant cash of their day.

SOCIAL SCIENCE EXPERIENCE

Concepts:

Travelers and nomads must carry universally acceptable units of exchange for use in the different economic systems in which they find themselves.

In nomadic cultures, wealth is transported in the form of jewelry.

Objectives:

To examine the basic and economic needs of a constantly moving people.

Activities:

Discuss the value of the golden chain, aside from its material worth.

Discuss the hazards of wearing all of your wealth on a trip.

Discuss different currencies, rates of exchange and economic systems.

List goods and services that have historically been used for exchange.

Discuss the advantage of an item of exchange that is accepted internationally.   Pay special attention to credit cards, their benefits and their drawbacks, for users and for merchants.

ART EXPERIENCE

Concept:

Repetition of shape and color create a unified pattern.

Objectives:

To create a chain with a repeating pattern of links.

To change a spiral into a series of circles.

To gain skill in wrapping, bending and cutting wire.

Activity:

Materials: Wax paper, 5' of medium soft wire, pliers, wire cutters, a 1/2" dowel, a wooden block with a saw cut in it, a "C" clamp.

Directions: Wrap wax paper around the dowel. Wrap wire in a tight spiral around the dowel, using pliers where necessary. Remove the dowel. Using wire cutters, snip each complete loop. Using the "C" clamp, clamp the wooden block to a table. Place one end of a wire loop in the saw cut groove in the block, and bend the other end to meet it. Continue adding loops and pinching them closed to form the links in a chain. Use the chain as a key or watch chain.

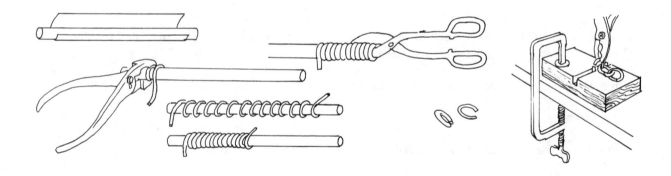

32. CELTIC REPOUSSE' (A)

In lands where a succession of invasions have occurred, such as Britain in the Bronze Age, cultures are affected in one of three ways: a) The cultures of the invaders and of the native population merge to form a common culture, often with elements surviving from both; b) The dominant culture of the invaders absorbs the local culture, which all but disappears; or c) The natives retreat from the invaders to save themselves, and in the process they preserve their own culture.

The Celts are an example of a culture that at various times and places did all three. In the parts of the world where the Celts themselves were the invaders, they melded with other cultures, leaving their stamp on most of northern Europe, especially in the Iberian Peninsula and Britain. In the face of invasion by the Danes, Angles, Romans and Saxons, the Celts withdrew and were able to retain their culture in remote areas of Scotland, Wales, Ireland and Brittany.

When not invading or being invaded, the Celts made a grand contribution to the mosaic of European civilization. They were inventors and innovators, developing advances in transportation, agriculture, economics, law, weaponry and metal-working. Iron was their favored medium. Archeologists in the United Kingdom and on the European continent have unearthed ironwork and many Celtic-made stone, bronze and, even, silver statues of figures depicted in action with complex textures and displaying a sophisticated decorative sense.

SOCIAL SCIENCE EXPERIENCE

Concept:

Now, as in history, craftmakers produce products for the use and enjoyment of their contemporaries. Their work is proof of their skill and artistry.

Objective:

To discover how craft objects are made, in order to better appreciate their makers' skill, the time in which the makers lived and the technology that was/is available to them.

Activities:

Study today's Celtic culture in the British Isles.

Research the Celtic influence on European culture.

Find other instances of cultural melding or survival.

Trace Celtic word origins in present-day English.

ART EXPERIENCE

Concept:

A progression from high to low relief can suggest the illusion of spatial depth.

Objectives:

To make a figured plaque in metal relief.

To imply depth in space by a progression from high to low relief.

To show a variety of textures.

To draw people and animals in simplified, decorative design forms.

Activity:

Materials: Heavy foil, wooden sticks with flat and pointed tips, a magazine, a sheet of thin paper, a pencil, tape.

Directions: On thin paper, draw figures to size.   Add indications of texture.   Place foil on the magazine.   Tape the sketch over the foil and trace the outlines of the figures.   To create a high relief effect, reverse the foil and rub the inside outline with the flat end of the stick. Make the nearer shapes higher than those that are placed in the background.   (The numbers in the diagram indicate levels of distance; high numbers are more distant.)   Texture the figures by drawing lines and making dots with the pointed end of the stick.   Mat the finished repousse' for display.

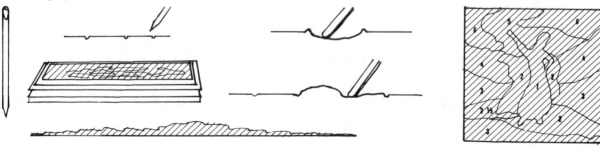

33. IRON SIGNS OF HAITI (B)

The Spanish and French colonists who settled the island of Haiti brought with them their languages, customs, and crafts, along with a huge population of imported African slaves. One craft in which both the French and the Spaniards excelled was iron-working. Spanish ironworkers produced wroughtiron church screens, lamps and similar furnishings, while the French crafted locks, bars and hardware. When the descendants of those early settlers won their independence from France in 1804, the craft of ironworking remained. But, like the natives of Trinidad who interpreted the French masques in their own way, the Haitians crafted ironwork to suit their own needs and culture.

Today, steel drums are a ready source of material for Haitian metalwork. The drums are cut apart and worked by punching, splitting and incising to create a distinctive island art form. Thus, the Haitian metalworkers have adapted European ironworking techniques to their own local materials and customs.

SOCIAL SCIENCE EXPERIENCE

Concept:

The advanced technologies of more sophisticated cultures often alter the methods and products of less structured cultures.

Objective:

To recognize the advantages to be gained by a culture's adoption of a new, improved technology; to recognize the kinds of disadvantages that also might result from the adoption.

Activities:

Explore the actual effects of new technology on several different cultures. Consider the technology's effects on the daily life, economy, and arts of the culture. (Suggestions: Inuits, the Cargo Cult of New Guinea, Aborigines in Australia.)

Learn about the French influence on Haiti.

Listen to steel drum band music from the Caribbean. Explain the origin of the steel drum.

Research pictures of European ironwork and compare its variety to examples in Haiti, New Orleans, and other "new world" locations.

ART EXPERIENCE

Concept:

The contrast of positive and negative areas defines shape.

Objectives:

To make a sign using silhouetted figures.

To create a balance between positive and negative space.

To simplify complex forms into silhouettes.

To increase skill in cutting.

Activity:

Materials: A black mat or poster board, a piece of sketch paper (as large as the mat or poster board), a pencil, a mat knife.

Directions: On the sketch paper draw a design, made up of negative and positive spaces. Keep within a border and connect all of the positive spaces either to the border or to each other. Cut out all of the negative spaces. Use the cutout as a stencil to transfer the design in reverse (flip the image) to the back of the board. (If lettering is included in the sign, the transfer must be made in reverse.) Place some padding under the board to protect the blade and the underlying work surface. Cut out the negative spaces. Finally, flip the board to view its front surface.

 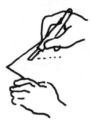  

34.   OAXACA TINPLATE (B)

Long before the 16th century when Hernando Cortez and the Spanish conquistadors set foot in Mexico, the native artisans of Central America were making sophisticated works in gold, silver and copper that even the equally great goldsmiths of Spain were forced to admire.   Originally, there was little mining of ores in Mexico: there was enough metal ore available on the surface to satisfy the needs of the inhabitants.   But along with the Spanish Conquest came demands to increase production, both of raw materials and finished products; and not only of gold and silver, but also of iron and tin.   Eventually pressures for increased production led to the development and use of metal alloys such as brass, and more recently, tinplate as substitutes for the more valuable materials.

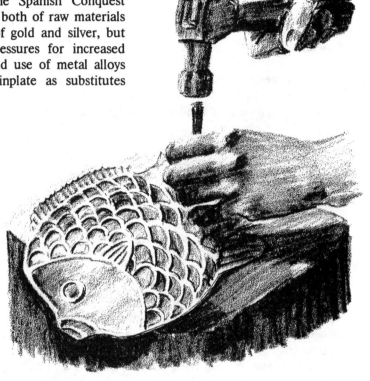

Today, tinplate is made from discarded tin cans combined with sheet brass.   It has various thicknesses and is worked, hammered, cut and pierced, much like copper.   The tinplate for creating ornaments is usually thinner than that used to make pots and pans.   Flowers, birds, insects and animals are the predominant subjects for the decorative tinplate pieces produced in Mexico today.   But tinplate has its practical uses, too.

SOCIAL SCIENCE EXPERIENCE

Concepts:

Artisans often employ a new, more efficient or less expensive technique or material to imitate a valued object.

Excessive demand for a product often leads to changed or relaxed quality standards.

Objective:

To recognize the particulars in the debate between two economic positions: 1) a product should be kept the same, even if doing so entails a rise in cost; or 2) a product's quality should be lowered in order to retain its original price.

Activities:

Evaluate three products weighing their aesthetic considerations against resource depletion and marketing considerations.

Determine the reasons for the value of gold, silver, copper, steel, tin.

Research the history of the tin can and its changeover to the aluminum can.   What are its features and benefits?

ART EXPERIENCE

Concept:

Organic design is often symmetrical. Symmetrical designs lend unity.

Objectives:

To make a metal plaque or picture.

To design a symmetrical biomorphic design with a complex texture.

To learn to develop a motif.

To practice working in reverse, impressing, cutting and piercing.

Activity:

Materials: An aluminum pie pan bottom (disposable), heavy-duty scissors, a hammer, a wooden block, a 20-penny common nail.

Directions: Cut off the side rim of pie pan. Trace an organic shape onto the plate bottom. Experiment with a nail on some metal scraps placed against the wooden block, piercing the scraps with the nail tip. Note that the holes punched in a row make lines and that the edge of the nail head may be tapped along a line to form an indentation. A raised design can be made by tapping on the reverse side. When the techniques are mastered, then start tapping the design onto the pie pan bottom. Hang the finished plaque or picture on the wall.

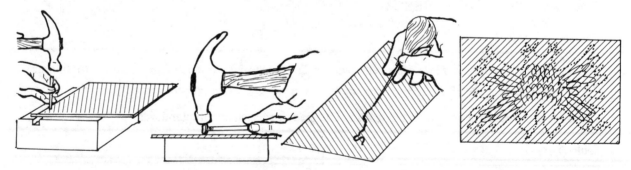

35. APACHE JINGLES (B)

The Apache Indians of the American Southwest have a traditional ceremonial dance for their young girls, to recognize and celebrate their coming of age. In accordance with Apache custom, each girl participating in the dance wears for the first time a special "camp dress" that is made for her by her mother and her aunts. The girl will wear the camp dress again many times during the ceremonial occasions of her tribal life.

A camp dress consists of a special buckskin blouse and skirt. They are entirely hand-sewn. Long fringes on the sleeves hang from shoulder to wrist. Rolled aluminum "jingles" are attached to these fringes, as well as to the hems of the blouse and skirt. When the wearer moves, the jingles touch together and make a soft, musical sound.

Today's aluminum jingles are substitutes for the shells that originally were used for camp dresses. The shells are said to have made a "soft swishing sound, as does the wind in the tall pine tress."

SOCIAL SCIENCE EXPERIENCE

Concept:

Artisans often employ a new, more efficient or inexpensive technique or material to imitate a valued object.

Objective:

To identify several new materials that have replaced hard-to-find or hard-to-work-with traditional materials.

Activities:

Discuss the uses of shell today, also the materials that have replaced shell as a basic material: i.e., plastic for mother-of-pearl inlay; metal for the "tattles" on tambourines; European mass produced beads for original wampum.

List other ways that dancers imitate natural phenomena, such as wind in the trees: swans, snowflakes, whirlwinds, snakes, cats.

Watch performances of world dances in person or on video. Identify movements that are imitations of natural phenomena. Note how sound, light, music are used to support the illusion.

Study other coming-of-age ceremonies in other cultures and compare them to contemporary customs.

ART EXPERIENCE

Concept:

Moving parts add emphasis, variety and visual interest.

Objectives:

To make a necklace or a mobile using beads and jingles made from aluminum cans.

To consciously use sound and movement as design elements.

To gain skill in cutting, piercing and rolling aluminum.

Activity:

Materials: Aluminum cans, heavy thread, scissors, a hammer, beads, a nail, a wooden block, bottle caps; branches, a 20" wire for a necklace (or dowels or coat hangers for a mobile).

Directions: Cut down the side of an aluminum can, by piercing and cutting it with scissors. Flatten the can into a sheet and trace a minimum of 24 circles on it, using bottle caps as templates. Cut out the circles. Use the nail to hammer a hole into each circle near its edge. (Hammer into the woodblock.) Then, roll the circles around a pencil, a nail or a wire. (Keep the holes at the top edge of the rolls.) Tie a thread through the hole in each aluminum "Jingle" roll and add beads as desired. Tie threads to the wire hanger pieces (dowels or sections of coat hanger wire), close enough so that the jingles will touch each other in a breeze, (if making a mobile). If making a necklace, tie the threads onto the wire about 1/2" apart and bend the ends of the wire back on themselves 1/2" to form a catch.

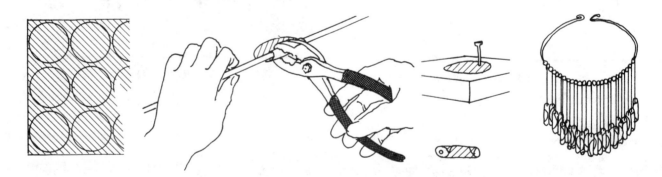

36. EGYPTIAN LINEAR GOLD DESIGN (C)

When British Egyptologist Howard Carter first peered into Tutankhamen's tomb in 1922, he remarked, "—strange animals, statues, and gold, . . .everywhere the glint of gold." He was surrounded by objects of gold, many more than had been found in previous tomb excavations, and their splendor and craftsmanship were unsurpassed. When Tutankhamen's treasure was exhibited in the United States (in 1976), modern-day viewers were no less awed by its luxury and beauty.

Among the artifacts in the tomb was a golden shrine nearly eight feet wide. (It held the young Pharaoh's canopic urns, ornate containers for his mummified vital organs.) On the doors of the shrine, a procession of deities welcomes Tutankhamen to the afterworld. The goddess Isis stretches her wings protectively across the sides of the shrine, framing its hieroglyphic inscriptions.

Goldsmiths were the most highly respected artisans in ancient Egypt. Perhaps the finest of them worked on Tutankhamen's shrine. The underlying structure is made of oak. It is thought that the relief designs were first worked into large sheets of gold. Next, the gold was turned face down and a layer of linen laid over its back. Then, gesso was poured over the linen, filling the depressions in the gold relief and forming an even surface. Finally, a second layer of linen was laid over the flat gesso surface. This gave the relief designs on the gold sheet a firm backing. Finally, the four-layered whole was fastened on to the wooden panels of the shrine. Intricate details may have been emphasized by further tapping after the gold was in place.

SOCIAL SCIENCE EXPERIENCE

Concept:

People are very curious about and place great value on art and craft objects from ancient civilizations.

Objective:

To identify the criteria by which people assign value to art and craft objects.

Activities:

Study the treasures found in Tutankhamen's tomb. Discuss the reasons (beyond material worth) for placing such high value on the objects.

Compare King Tut's ancient toys with those of today's 12 year olds.

Compare ancient Egyptian burial customs to contemporary practices. Study the mummification process.

Look at X-rays of mummies. Discuss the significance of the X-rays. Visit the X-ray section of a local hospital and learn the significance of X-rays for living people.

Design an Egyptian tomb and list items that should be buried in it.

Study "Egyptomania" throughout history Napoleonic France, Victorian England, 1920's America, 1970's America.

ART EXPERIENCE

Concept:

Lines are essential design elements for defining shapes, patterns and textures.

Objectives:

To make a design in relief, working both sides of metal foil.

To learn incising and embossing skills.

Activity:

Materials: Heavy aluminum foil or gold metallic board, a magazine, a sharp-pointed wooden dowel, felt, tracing paper.

Directions: On tracing paper, sketch the outline of a design and indicate linear textures and patterns. Cover a magazine with a piece of felt. Lay the foil (or board) on the felt and tape the sketch on top. Trace the outline of the sketch into the foil with the dowel. Remove the sketch and draw in textures and patterns using repetitive dots and lines.

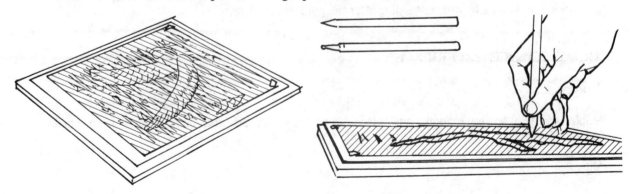

37. IVORY COAST WIRECRAFTING (C)

The Ivory Coast Republic is a small African country that borders the Gulf of Guinea. The people of the Ivory Coast are Ashanti in language and custom. In pre-colonial times, the Ashanti gained wealth through trading and gold-mining. Today, they still trade and export cocoa.

The craftspeople of the Ivory Coast make small golden treasures for trade throughout the world. Each distinctive human or animal figure begins as a carefully modeled clay figure which is covered with coiled and interlaced soft wire, and held together with beads of solder. When completed, the wire and clay figure is covered with another layer of clay and then fired. The firing hardens both layers of clay and melts away the wire inside them, leaving a hollow mold. The mold is then filled with melted gold (which cools in the shape of the melted away wire). Finally, the clay mold is broken to reveal the unique gold figure that has formed inside.

SOCIAL SCIENCE EXPERIENCE

Concept:

Crafts made for trade are an important economic supplement to agricultural products, the exploitation of natural resources and tourism, the usual economic mainstays of non-industrial countries.

Objectives:

To recognize the impact of crafts and cottage industries on agrarian societies.

Activities:

Take charge of an imaginary non-industrial country. Set up a viable cottage industry product. Discuss the materials, the skills, the equipment needed for production; also discuss marketing plans: possibilities and limitations.

Discuss the benefits of an oil discovery to an impoverished country; also cite the drawbacks. Determine which members of the population would feel the effects of the discovery right away and later; consider what would happen if the wells suddenly went dry.

ART EXPERIENCE

Concept:

The repetition and placement of lines can build up mass.

Objectives:

To make a small wire pin using wire coiling and wrapping techniques.

To define shape by the use of positive and negative space.

To develop variety in texture by varying linear elements.

To gain skill in precision gluing.

Activity:

Materials: Copper or aluminum wire, strong glue, a pin back, wire snips.

Directions: Draw the design of a pin. Bend an outline of the shape of the piece. Then, bend and/or weave its other design features and glue them inside the wire outline. Work on an oily surface to avoid gluing the pieces to the table. (To make the design features, experiment with bending the wire, weaving it as mesh and coiling it into spirals. Features can be trimmed to fit the design after they are glued together.)

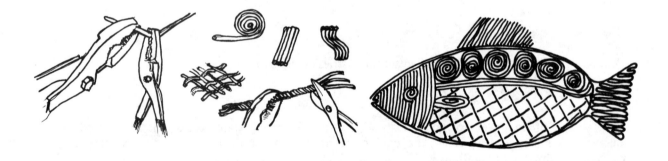

38. MINOAN FOIL REPOUSSE' (C)

Around 7000 B.C. (the Neolithic Period) the Minoan civilization arose on the island of Crete where it flourished unhampered and developed into an advanced Bronze Age culture, around 3500 B.C., well ahead of its contemporaries.

Today, archeologists are able to study the remains of four great palaces on the island, at Knossos, Mallia, Phaistos, and Zakro. Even as ruins, all are grand in size and provide elegant glimpses of Minoan architecture. Most of our knowledge of Minoan culture comes from the painted frescos and clay, stone, bronze, and precious metal art objects found at these sites. Minoan artists depicted people engaged in activities both serious and commonplace, such as performing athletic feats, enacting religious rituals or, simply, catching fish.

Pins, brooches, rings, and other small pieces delighted wealthy Minoans.   Their jewelry shows evidence of delicate craftsmanship, including raised and incised designs of marvelous intricacy.   Their creations are detailed and sophisticated, and feature abstractions of form and texture.   Minoan craftsmen understood how to create the illusion of three-dimensional space to indicate distance.   They made use of such spatial devices as varying the relative sizes of figures and blurring details to indicate distance.

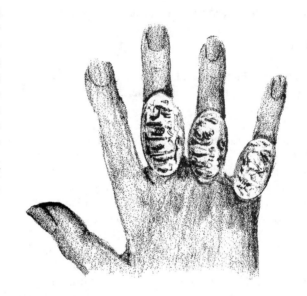

SOCIAL SCIENCE EXPERIENCE

Concept:

Because detailed written records about most ancient civilizations do not exist, information about them is deduced from their utilitarian and decorative objects.

Objective:

To recognize that every object, whether historic or contemporary, presents clues about the people who make, use or value the object.

Activities:

Discuss why jewelry, paintings, and other artifacts with pictorial content are important clues to the past.

Generalize about why jewelry would be important to historical research.   What does jewelry tell about an individual? about the culture in which the individual lives?   about the culture which produced the piece of jewelry?

Locate Crete on a map and learn about Minoan culture.

Study Minoan frescos and goldwork.

ART EXPERIENCE

Concept:

A progression from low to high relief can suggest depth and dimensionality in a piece of craft-work.

Objectives:

To make a medallion of heavy foil with a representational scene on it.

To develop skill in suggesting dimensionality by showing different spatial planes.

To develop skills in repousse', raising metal, and in texturing.

Activity:

Materials: Heavy metal foil, a 1/4" dowel (sharpened on one end and sanded flat on the other), tracing paper, tape, a magazine, a chain or chord (to hang the medallion), cardboard, glue and a hole punch.

Directions: On tracing paper draw a scene within a 2" circle. Use at least three spatial planes. Place a sheet of foil on a magazine (for padding). Tape the tracing paper drawing on top of the foil and, using the dowel, draw (transfer) a line around the outer edge of the circle. Use the circle as a guide to draw a larger 2.5" circle around the first one. Next, use the dowel to transfer the outlines of the scene. (Take special care not to pierce the foil.) Do not texture or add much detail. Remove the tracing paper and clarify the outlines on the foil. Then, reverse the foil and draw lines just inside of the original lines (which are now "outlines" because now they stand "out") to reinforce the repousse' effect. To make larger areas stand out, rub the back of the foil with the flat end of the dowel. Make sure to do the foreground figures first, creating the highest relief. Continue in order of distance away from the foreground. Finally, add texture (small, repetitive dots and lines) and other details.

Cut out the 2.5" circle. Then, make a 2" cardboard circle. Punch a hole about 1/4" from its edge. Carefully lay the foil circle over the cardboard one. Don't flatten the design. Make sure the hole in the cardboard is exactly placed behind the top, center of the foil design. Then, pierce the foil to match the hole in the cardboard. Fold back and glue the foil edge all around the cardboard circle. Tie the chain or chord through the hole.

39. TURKOMAN HAND SET (C)

Turkoman tribes, once nomadic, still inhabit the Amu Darya River valley that extends southward from the Aral Sea, through the Uzbek and Turkmen Soviet Socialist Republics, and to the northern border of Afghanistan. Today, most Turkomans have settled into permanent locales, where they work the land or practice crafts. However, many of their nomadic traditions still persist. One such custom is the wearing of "portable wealth" in the form of silver coins and trinkets. The jewelry is worn by the women of the tribe, who according to tradition, accumulate family wealth through dowries, gifts and inheritances, as well as through other sources of income. The women proudly display their family fortunes. Among the Turkoman people, there is little doubt as to who is wealthy and who isn't.

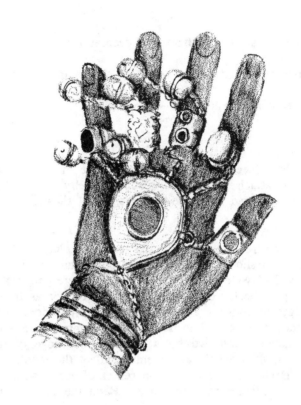

One interesting kind of Turkoman jewelry is worn on the hands. It consists of a bracelet linked to a brooch and to rings by short chains. All are embellished with jewels, beads and bells.

SOCIAL SCIENCE EXPERIENCE

Concept:

The use of traditional craft objects may persist despite obsolescence, because they perpetrate traditional values and embody meaning for a changing culture.

Objectives:

To compare and contrast the ways that family wealth is conserved.

To conduct research on dowry customs in various cultures.

To learn about nomadic lifestyles in modern times, especially about nomads who regularly cross international boundaries.

Activities:

Review the present state of relations between Afghanistan and the U.S.S.R.

Research the use of hand jewelry (especially rings); their purposes, their symbolism; from ancient Rome to Ringo, from signets to cigar bands.

ART EXPERIENCE

Concept:

Graduated shapes unify form. Moving parts add emphasis, variety and visual interest.

Objectives:

To make a "hand set" with textured decorations.

To unify the hand set by repeating shapes in graduated sizes, from the bracelet to the rings.

To increase incising and metal-cutting skills.

Activity:

Materials: Sheet copper (about 20 square inches per set), a copper chain, "jump" rings (open circles to attach pieces), old costume jewelry (or beads and bells), a nail, a nail set (used to set the nail head into wood), pliers, metal shears, an electric drill with a small bit, fine emery paper, glue.

Directions: Make paper patterns for a bracelet 1 1/4" wide by the circumference of the wrist. The pattern should include a teardrop medallion (1 1/2" long by 1" wide), 5 finger rings (3" long by 3/4" wide at their centers and tapered to 1/4" at their ends). Fit the patterns onto the copper sheet, using the edge of the copper as the edge for the bracelet, and common-cut the edges to conserve copper and reduce the amount of cutting. Mark bands of the design on the bracelet piece and incise it with a hammer and a nail. (Use a nail set or engraving tool, if available.) Drill two holes on the lower edge of the bracelet, 1" from either side of the center. Drill one hole at the small end of the teardrop brooch and five holes along its bottom edge. Drill one hole at the top center of each ring. Decorate the bracelet with the medallion, and the medallion with the rings. Bend the bracelet and the rings to fit the wrist and hand.

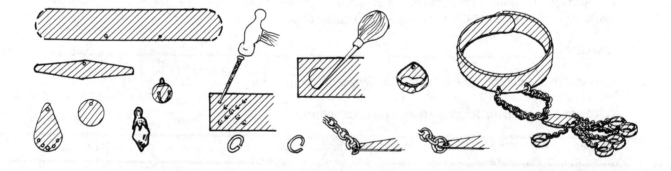

5

DYES, YARNS, BEADS AND THREADS

40. CREE BEADWORK (A)

Much like their ancestors, Canada's Cree Indians live a rugged life close to the land.   They still fish, hunt and tan hides by hand, to make clothes for themselves and others in the tribe.

Cree decorative quillwork has been judged among the finest in North America.   But, due to both the scarcity of (and the difficulty in working with) quills, today's Cree artisans use trade beads which are readily available and offer variety in color and style.

The Cree adorn soft leather garments, especially mittens and moccasins, with intricate beadwork patterns.   The mittens often feature floral designs.   In use, they are attached to each end of a plaited thong (which hangs around the neck inside the wearer's coat).   The thong keeps the mittens "handy" and prevents their loss.   Cree beadworkers also decorate other kinds of leather goods which they sell.

SOCIAL SCIENCE EXPERIENCE

Concept:

To imitate a rare and valued object, artisans often employ a new, more efficient or less expensive material or technique.

Objectives:

To recognize and examine the motives and purposes of art and craft production in a culture.

To identify the qualities in the lifestyles of a culture which will allow for the production of art and craft pieces.

To recognize the difference between utility and decoration.   To explore instances in which the two qualities are combined.

Activities:

Collect examples of inexpensive materials that replace the use of natural materials from animal, vegetable and/or mineral sources.   (Examples: plastic-handled knives instead of bone-handled ones; acrylic yarn for vegetable-dyed wool; teflon or aluminum cooking pans instead of cast-iron ones.)   Explain the rationale for the replacement.

Estimate how much food will be required to make sure there will be enough for the class to eat for a week.   Discuss how much time and what kind of tools it would take for class members to provide the food they will need for a week.   Discuss what the class members will do in their spare time after they secure their food supply for a week.

ART EXPERIENCE

Concept:

Contrasts in color or texture add variety and emphasis.

Objectives:

To make a beaded pendant.

To create a symmetrical design with one dominant shape.

To create texture by organization of bead rows.

To contrast colors for design emphasis.

To gain skill in beadwork.

Activity:

Materials: A chamois skin (polishing cloth) or piece of heavy felt, trade beads in many colors, a needle, thread, a thimble, tracing paper, a soft-leaded pencil, scissors.

Directions: On tracing paper, with a soft pencil, make a symmetrical floral or geometric design, about 2 1/2" x 5". Use the pencil to blacken the back of the paper. Then, redraw/transfer the design onto the chamois (felt). To start the beadwork, bring thread up through the chamois, from the unmarked side, and insert the needle through the first bead. Secure the bead by sewing down through the design, pulling the thread tight, then bringing the thread up, through the bead and down through the chamois once again (in the same place as the first stitch). The rest of the beads can be sewn in groups of three or four. Be sure to secure the last bead with double stitches (as with the first).

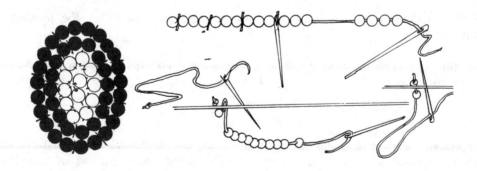

41. MING GOLD EMBROIDERY (A)

It has been said that "clothes make the man"—or woman. Nowhere could it have been more true than in the China of the Ming Dynasty (1368-1644). Silks, heavy and light, were the textiles of choice for the wealthy and powerful. Heavy embroidery was used to identify official rank, much as the modern day military uses chevron stripes, stars and other symbols. As they advanced in rank, Ming officials added embroidered "mandarin squares" to their robes, as symbols of both civil and military authority. Only the Emperor was allowed to wear all twelve mandarin squares.

One method of protecting the delicate silk of the garment was to embroider the motifs separately on stiff gauze or paper. The finished patch was then appliqued to the garment. This method also served to hide the "wrong side" stitches, because the back of the patch was never visible.

The gold and silk embroideries of the Orient have influenced European needleworkers since the days of Marco Polo. Today, the embroidered work of both Orientals and Europeans is treasured and conserved by religious organizations, museums and textile collections worldwide.

SOCIAL SCIENCE EXPERIENCE

Concept:

Clothing styles and decorations often are used to display symbols of membership, rank and/or power.

Objective:

To recognize and explore the reasons for the use of symbols worn on clothing to convey messages.

Activities:

Describe different ways to indicate occupation, wealth, social position or authority in clothing.

List professions, organizations and personal ideas that use uniforms, pins or badges as symbols of their identity or belief.

Design an embroidered patch or uniform for a fantasy organization, rank or other purpose. (Example: Translator of alien languages on Spaceship ZX200.)

ART EXPERIENCE

Concept:

Closely-placed straight lines can be grouped and varied to produce varieties in shape, texture and pattern.

Objectives:

To embroider and applique' a patch onto a T-shirt or other item of clothing.

To create a design with varied groups of straight lines and contrasting colors.

To vary the direction of lines to define shape and add texture.

To learn to "couch," by oversewing threads or fibers onto a fabric.

Activity:

Materials: Medium weight cloth, heavy paper, metallic cord, embroidery floss, a needle, a thimble, an embroidery hoop.

Directions: Draw a design on paper. Place the paper on top of cloth and lock both into the embroidery hoop. Use a threaded needle to follow the design and work through the paper and cloth. Outline the shapes with heavy thread or cord and oversew to hold them in place on the fabric. Then use embroidery floss and the satin stitch to fill in the other areas of color. Applique the finished patch to a sash, headband, sleeve of a T-shirt or a flag.

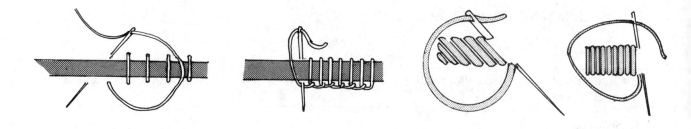

42. SILKEN CHAINS OF CHINESE TAPESTRY (A)

In ancient China, long before the invention of modern mechanical looms capable of weaving programmed designs, needleworkers produced fine hand-embroidered silks that are still admired today as rich multi-colored works of art. Birds and rocks, clouds and water, the wonders of nature, as well as tiny human figures were intertwined in detailed designs composed of thousands of tiny stitches. Often the subject matter was complex, yet all of it was done using a simple chain stitch. This historic stitch is still in vogue as a method of stitchery. It was the first stitch produced by sewing machines and continues to be used for some of today's industrial stitching.

The ancient Chinese embroiderers began by outlining areas of color on their silk cloths, then patiently working rows of stitches inside the outlines until the areas were covered. The method was simple, but effective. Even in the earliest times metallic threads were used. The shimmering threads added "life" to the writhing dragons, swimming carp and shining armor pictured on the silken garments of the courtiers.

SOCIAL SCIENCE EXPERIENCE

Concept:

Superior design and craftsmanship in garments can reach the level and value of an art form.

Objectives:

To examine the fine line between craft and art.

Activities:

Study masterpieces of embroidery throughout history and in various cultures.

Compare the amounts of time it takes to produce finished products in several different craft forms. Which take more or less time than embroidery? Determine the relationship between time spent to produce a product and the value of the product.

ART EXPERIENCE

Concept:

Areas within a design gain unity through the repetition of color, shapes and textures.

Objectives:

To embroider a scene or figure using the basic chain stitch.

To create vibrant color contrasts.

To maintain unity by repetition of the shape and texture of stitches.

Activity:

Materials: A 10" fabric square, an embroidery hoop, embroidery floss in (at least) three colors plus black and white, a needle, a thimble, a pencil.

Directions: Design a scene or figure that can be outlined and has at least three repetitions of shape. Blacken the back of the design with a pencil, then transfer the design to the fabric (by tracing over the design's outlines). Leave a 2" border on all sides. Secure the fabric in the embroidery hoop. Then use the chain stitch to outline the shapes. Fill in the outlined areas with rows of chain stitching in one or more colors. Avoid having the same colors adjoining; if one color does touch itself in the next area, then stitch outlines between them in black or white.

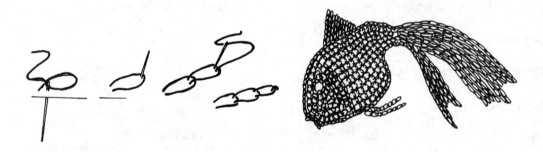

43. THE STORY-TELLING ROBE OF HUNAN (A)

Long ago, in the province of Hunan, China, there lived a wealthy lady named Ch'ang O. When her tomb was opened in modern times, archeologists unearthed many beautiful things: lacquered dishes, carved teak chests, musical instruments and jewelry in boxes with hand-carved dragons on the lids. Perhaps, most remarkable of all was a ceremonial robe embroidered with the story of Ch'ang O's journey through life.

The robe depicts Ch'ang O stealing the elixir of immortality and flying to the moon on a dragon's wings. The robe also shows her husband shooting false suns with magic arrows, leaving only the true one in its place in the heavens. The sun and the moon represent Yang and Yin, the universal opposites in Chinese philosophy. Another scene shows Ch'ang O passing between two red leopard guards as she enters Heaven's Gate.

The robe has an almost symmetrical design that includes many dragons. It is embroidered in red, brown, blue, green black and white, and is embellished with green tassels hanging from the sleeves.

SOCIAL SCIENCE EXPERIENCE

Concept:

Many cultures hold the belief that personal possessions may accompany the dead into the after-life.

Objective:

To examine some of the varied conceptions about mortality and immortality held by cultures throughout the world.

Activities:

Discuss the desire for immortality and our own culture's attitudes toward aging, death and burial.

Learn about ancient burial customs.

Study Chinese mythology and research the meaning of Yin and Yang.

Compare the treasures found in Ch'ang O's tomb with those found in the burials of Egyptian and Celtic princesses; Egyptian and Anglo-Saxon kings.

ART EXPERIENCE

Concept:

A symmetrical design is a balance of similar and/or equal visual units on either side of a center point or axis.

Objectives:

To make a story-telling robe with a symbolic message.

To plan the thematic unity of the entire design, and balance the design symmetrically.

To create harmony of shape and color.

To learn enlarging and pattern-making skills.

To exercise drawing, painting and sewing skills.

Activity:

Materials: Large drawing paper, an old sheet or cloth, colored crayons, a yardstick, scissors.

Directions: On paper, draw a scale pattern of a design with a "T" shape, 18" high, 10" wide at the bottom, 18" wide at the top, and 6" deep across the top. Cut the pattern out, making a small oval cut at the top (for the neck) and a slit down the front (for access).

Next, draw a symmetrical story-design on the pattern paper. Cut a neck opening in the sheet (as shown in the diagram) and cut the excess fabric away from the sleeves. Fold the design and the cloth into proportionately equal sections. Then, draw the enlarged design onto cloth, a section at a time. Use crayons to color all of the story elements on the robe. Sew under the sleeves and down the sides. Fasten the front with pins.

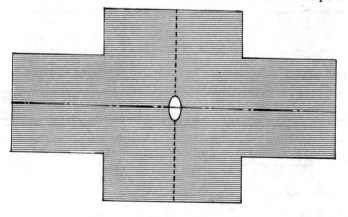

44. BATTOCHES, THE DECORATED LEATHER BOXES OF NIGER (A)

Artisan families of Niger in north central Africa make beautifully-crafted leather boxes called "battoches." The boxes are made from untanned hides, and are traditionally decorated with geometric patterns. Battoches are used to hold cosmetics, jewelry, perfumes, and other precious possessions.

Battoche-making begins with the forming of a hollow clay mold. The mold is dusted with chalk and wrapped with a water-soaked animal skin. (The skin has been shaved thin to allow it to stretch and shape easily.) The pieces of skin, for the bottom of the box, are fitted over the mold and to each other at the same time, and then allowed to dry. Next, the box is decorated with beeswax warmed in the hot sun. The soft wax is pressed into the leather to make resist designs. Several applications of dye are poured over the box and allowed to dry. The wax design strips are then removed, and a pattern emerges where the wax has resisted the dye. Finally, the box is tapped to break the clay mold inside and release the box and its lid for use.

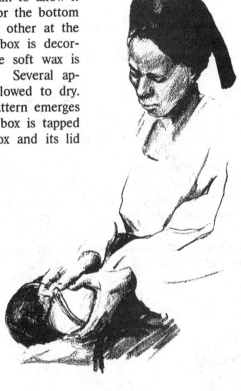

SOCIAL SCIENCE EXPERIENCE

Concept:

Cultures with few resources make creative uses of those resources.

Objective:

To compare the qualities of functional and aesthetic craft items.

Activities:

Locate Niger on a map. Speculate from its location why leather is the material used by the battoche-makers. Investigate the actual lifestyle of the people and find facts to explain why they use leather.

Compare the battoche and the decorated calabash for size, uses, designs, and cost of production. Study other wax-resist methods of dyeing, such as batik and Ukrainian Easter eggs.

ART EXPERIENCE

Concept:

Linear design can accentuate shape.

Objectives:

To decorate a patch of leather for applique' onto a garment or for use as a coaster or luggage tag.

To emphasize the shape of the leather patch by using lines and geometric patterns.

To contrast the design pattern with the dyed background.

Activity:

Materials: Leather shapes (approximately 4" x 4"), a knife, beeswax, cold water dye, a bowl, a teaspoon, a heat lamp or a spotlight.

Directions: Warm the wax under a light (or lamp) until it is soft and workable. Shape the wax into long, thin strips by rolling under fingertips and applying medium pressure. Following the line of the design, press the still-warm wax onto the leather. Then spoon dye over the leather several times, while catching the drain-off in a bowl. Put the leather in a refrigerator and, when cold, crack or scrape off the wax. Sew the leather onto a garment, to serve as a decoration, or coat it with wax, for use as a coaster, or punch a hole near the edge and write a name and address on it, for use as a luggage tag.

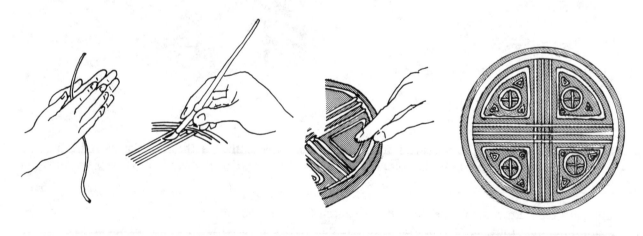

45. INUIT WALL HANGINGS (A)

The work of contemporary Inuit artists is vital and direct. It uses new materials, made available in the Arctic only through trade, yet retains traditional ideas and forms. For example, traded woolen goods have been combined with indigenous fur and skin to create modern garments. The bright colors dyed into wools and yarns are not natural in hides nor are they part of the Inuit tradition. However, the designs on the new, colorful garments are still derived from the customary design motifs used in Inuit folk carvings.

Wall hangings are a new art form for the Inuit, and are made as an item for trade, to exchange for new products and materials from the South. The subjects for the wall hangings are drawn from daily life, but the artists do not try to maintain a fixed perspective or a visual story line. Rather, bold and simple shapes, textures and color contrasts are combined to make the hangings visually striking.

SOCIAL SCIENCE EXPERIENCE

Concept:

Cultures grow and change by adapting new ideas and materials to traditional products and activities.

Objective:

To recognize the positive and negative results of cross cultural influences.

Activities:

Discuss how the once-isolated Inuit culture has been affected by the influx of technology from America and Canada.

Define and compare the concepts of primitive and modern cultures. Do Inuit people fit the definition of a primitive people? Or are they modern?

Find examples of modern technology's influence on once primitive cultural groups. Try to identify as many positive improvements and as many negative detriments as possible.

Evaluate how crafts improve the Inuit (or any other) economy.

ART EXPERIENCE

Concept:

The simplification of three-dimensional form and texture into two-dimensional shape produces a powerful design.

Objectives:

To make an Inuit-style wall hanging.

To simplify the shapes of figures and objects.

To pay attention to balance in asymmetrical design.

To create texture with yarn.

To learn felt marking, cutting and embroidery stitches (back stitch and buttonhole stitch).

Activity:

Materials: Felt (for the background), assorted felt pieces, wool yarn, a yarn needle, scissors, pins, chalk, white glue, hanging rings, heavy paper.

Directions: On paper draw the outlines of figures in characteristic positions. Omit small details. Cut out the figures. Use chalk to trace the outlines of the figures onto the felt pieces. Cut out enough figures to fill the background felt.   Arrange the figures on the felt around its center. Mark the place of each figure with chalk. Remove, one at a time, and use sewn-on yarn to add texture or decoration to each figure. Glue the finished figures in place on the background. Then buttonhole stitch around the outside of the hanging. To prepare for hanging, sew rings along the upper edge of the felt background.

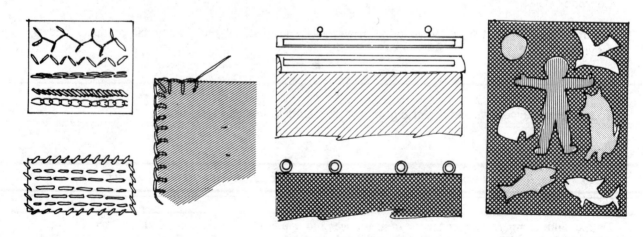

46. PRESSURE-DYED PATTERNS OF BENIN (B)

Indigo producing plants are still widely cultivated on every continent (except Australia). The source of the beautiful dark, indigo blue dyestuff is the flower of the liana vine family. Until the modern introduction of synthetic dyes, natural indigo was the most widely used cloth dye. However, it is not color fast, and often imparts a bluish cast to the skin of wearers of indigo-dyed garments. Modern chemistry has now developed a wide range of colorfast indigo (and other hues) for dyers to use on fabrics.

Benin, a small African nation formerly known as Dahomey, is situated on the Gold Coast of Africa. As such, Benin has had its share of European and Asian influences. The Europeans brought interesting fabric patterns and the Asians brought dye-resist techniques that influenced the native craftspeople. The dyers of Benin dig outdoor dye pits big enough to hold 40 pounds of dye and potash in 400 gallons of water. The mixture is allowed to ferment in the hot sun. Then, dampened cloth is dipped into the dye until the color reaches a desired intensity. After its removal from the dye pit, the cloth is dried in the sun.

Benin's traditional fabrics are sometimes tie-dyed into complex patterns that rival imported prints. Tie-dying is a pressure-resist technique, whereas batik is a wax-resist technique. In both, the dye does not penetrate the treated areas of the fabric. Instead, in the tied or waxed areas, intricate patterns emerge in the color(s) of the fabric, before its last color bath.

SOCIAL SCIENCE EXPERIENCE

Concept:

The availability of natural resources is the prime influence on the methods and types of craft products created by the people in a culture.

Objective:

To name some natural resources and list the types of crafts created from them; to name some craft forms and list the natural resources required to produce them.

Activities:

Name several different types of fabric-dying processes used in various cultures in the world.

Compare the costs and features of fabric that is decorated by hand and fabric that is decorated by machine; compare the value of each.

Study the great variety of African dyed fabrics.

ART EXPERIENCE

Concept:

A monochromatic color scheme is unifying.

Objectives:

To make a tie-dyed fabric.

To develop unity by using a single color and repeated pattern to fill an entire fabric.

To use sewing, tying and wrapping skills to create a pressure-resist dying pattern.

Activity:

Materials: White cotton cloth (2' square), dye, a basin, rubber gloves, a stick, yellow chalk, cotton balls, a needle, "button and carpet" thread, a thimble, scissors, clothes pins, drying wire.

Directions: Use yellow chalk to draw a large design on the cloth.   Sew and wrap rows of cotton balls along the lines of the pattern, as shown in the diagram.   Work out-of-doors, if possible, or cover all surfaces to protect them from drips.   Prepare the dye bath according to the package instructions.   Immerse the cloth in the dye using rubber gloves.   Stir with a stick. Fix the dye according to the instructions.   Remove threads.   Hang up the cloth to dry with clothespins.   Iron and applique' the design onto a pillow cover or a tote bag.

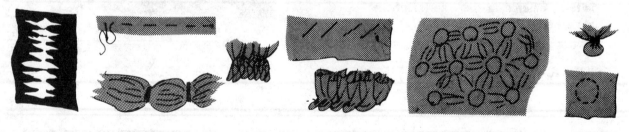

47. PATCHWORK OF AMERICAN SETTLERS (B)

The early settlers in the United States respected the maxim, "waste not, want not." Because the decorative chintz quilts of their European heritage were unavailable and they needed warm bedclothes, the early settlers began to piece together scraps of fabric to create patchwork quilts. The patterns that emerged, "Log Cabin," "Wedding Ring," "Courthouse Steps," were named for the experiences and surroundings that inspired their creators. Today, these traditional quilt patterns are collected as folk art.

Quilting became a social activity with the advent of the "quilting bee" which also had a practical benefit, in that because so many participated in the activity, the time required to produce a finished quilt was shortened markedly. Patchwork quilts customarily were presented by guests as bridal gifts. Four- and nine-patch blocks were combined with endless variety. Patchwork has grown more popular with time, and today clubs often make quilts to sell for fundraising. The recent popularity of patchwork may come from the increasing use of sewing machines, the relative ease with which the quilting can be accomplished and the accessibility of materials.

SOCIAL SCIENCE EXPERIENCE

Concept:

Cooperation makes labor-intensive tasks easier and quicker.

Objective:

To consider the variety of labor modes available for producing items; to recognize the features, benefits and/or liabilities of each mode in relation to specific production needs.

Activities:

List labor-intensive tasks that thrive on cooperation. Include some from the past (barn-raising) and from your life (house chores). Identify paid and unpaid, shared tasks.

Form a group to do a project for the school: make a quilt to sell or raffle; plan a bake sale; paint a peeling wall; produce a play.

ART EXPERIENCE

Concept:

The repetition of simplified shapes produces a unified pattern.

Objectives:

To cooperate in making a quilt block.

To simplify shapes to make a design.

To emphasize motif through value or color contrast.

To unify designs through repetitions of shapes and colors.

To gain skills in cutting and pattern-making.

Activity:

Materials: Printed and plain gift-wrapping paper, scissors, a ruler, poster board, paste, printed and plain fabric, a needle, thread, a thimble.

Directions: Use the ruler to draw a geometric patchwork design to fit inside a 12" square. Measure and cut the wrapping paper to fit the design. Cut out wrapping paper pieces and paste them onto the poster board (for reinforcement), leaving a 1/4" border around each piece. Cut along the outer edge of the border (to create reinforced pattern pieces). Lay the pieces on the fabric, trace around them with a pencil and, then, cut out the fabric pieces. Sew the edges of the pieces together, joining the 1/4" seams. Finally, sew the assembled fabric design onto a piece of solid colored fabric. Use the finished block as a pillow face or a wall hanging.

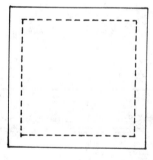 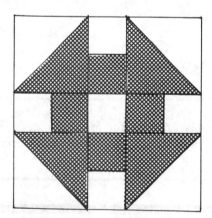 

48.   UKRAINIAN PSANKY (B)

Psanky, practiced in the Ukraine and eastern Europe, is the decoration of eggshells with wax-resist and dyes. Traditionally, the finished eggs are treasured gifts, exchanged between loved ones and friends after Easter services. They are crowded with symbols of the Easter celebration, and of bounty, prosperity and good wishes.

The psanky process begins three weeks before Easter with the preparation of the eggs. Because boiled eggs often crack and "blown" eggs do not immerse well, psanky eggs are usually raw, simply left to dry up inside over a period of time. After the drying, a wax design is applied to the outside of the eggshell with a "kistka," a pointed brass cone with a wooden handle. Beeswax is shaved into the cone of the kistka and melted over a candle. The decorator draws wax lines wherever the dye is not wanted. The egg is then dipped into a light color. More wax is applied, wherever the light color is to be protected. Successively darker colors are added, one by one, until the last, which is usually black.

SOCIAL SCIENCE EXPERIENCE

Concept:

Traditional craft items are often associated with holidays, celebrations or gift-giving occasions.

Objective:

To consider and explain the connection between gift-giving and special occasions.

Activities:

List craft traditions that are associated with holidays: Christmas cookies, Halloween pumpkins, Japanese kites.

Research gift-giving customs of other cultures.

Consider the difference between practical and impractical gifts.   Explain circumstances under which one or the other would be preferred.

ART EXPERIENCE

Concept:

Unity is gained through color and motif.

Objectives:

To decorate an egg with a symbolic picture-message.

To learn to apply cumulative layers of color.

To gain unity through the use of a single motif and variations.

To practice skills of designing, drawing with the kistka, and dyeing.

Activity:

Materials: Eggs, a pot of beeswax, a pan of water, a kistka or a substitute, a candle, food colors, a soft sponge, tissues, a dipper, a table knife, a hot plate. (Because boiled eggs often spot in dyeing, raw eggs can be used. They will dry up inside in a year or so.)

Directions: Clean the eggs and let them dry. Place a pot of beeswax in a pan of water, and heat it on a burner. Sketch a motif on paper. Define the distinct shapes to be dyed, from the lightest to the darkest color. Use analogous colors (yellow, yellow orange, orange, orange red et cetera), as each application of dye affects the colors that come after it. Apply wax to the areas where the white color of the egg shell will show. Dip the egg into the lightest color. Then, cover the area of this first color with wax (to preserve it), and dip the egg into the next color. Repeat until all of the colors have been dyed, waxed and dried. Warm the egg over a candle to remove the excess melted wax, taking care not to scorch the shell. Polish with tissues.

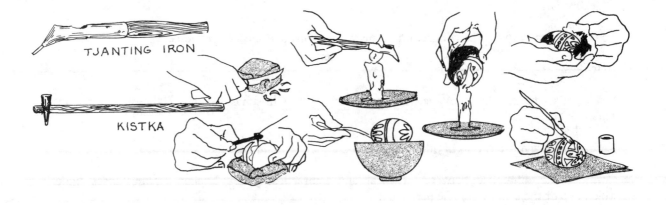

TJANTING IRON

KISTKA

49. AKHA ORNAMENTAL HEADBANDS (C)

The Akha tribespeople live in farming villages high in the mountains of northern Laos and Thailand. They are descended from the nomadic Mongols who live to the north. Formerly nomads themselves, the Akha retain the custom of displaying family wealth in the form of metallic ornamentations which are worn by their women.

Akha women wear distinctive headbands that display various combinations of beads, bells, discs, coins, hammered ornaments and tassels. The size of their heads and the twists of their hair are the only limits to the number of headbands the women can wear at any time. Sometimes additional, matching strands of beads are worn around the women's necks.

SOCIAL SCIENCE EXPERIENCE

Concept:

People in nomadic cultures often wear their wealth as ornamentation.

Objective:

To compare the cultural behaviors—regarding wealth of various kinds of cultures (nomads, subsistence farmers, hunters, technocrats and others).

Activities:

Gather data on the sources of income of a tribe in Thailand.

Identify and rank, in order of value, ten or more of the possessions of families in our culture.

Examine reasons why nomads, subsistence farmers and people in our own culture would invest in ornamentation.

ART EXPERIENCE

Concept:

Unity is gained through repetition of shape.

Objectives:

To make a beaded headband.

To select beads to create a harmony of color and shape.

To gain unity by the repetition of pattern.

To learn "couching" and sewing.

Activity:

Materials: A measuring tape, chalk, dark stretch fabric, a new pencil with an eraser, pins, cardboard, a needle and thread, beads, elastic, scissors, a thimble.

Directions: Measure for the correct head size, adding 1" to the length of the measurement (for a seam allowance). Double the fabric and cut it to the required length. Sew up the long side (doubled, on the wrong side), leaving a 1/2" seam allowance. Turn the fabric inside out, using a pencil eraser. Insert elastic for a better fit, if needed. Tape or pin the band to a piece of cardboard. Use chalk to mark the lines where each strand of beads will be placed. Large beads may be sewn individually. Couch on strands by sewing through the material and over the strand. Leave 1" at the fabric ends for sewing together as a seam. Sew the ends together by turning one end of the fabric inside itself (about 1/2"), then insert the other end, adjust the size until the band fits, and slip stitch the two ends together.

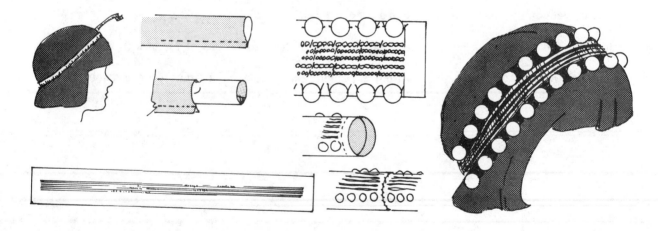

50. SEMINOLE PATCHWORK (C)

In the 1830's, the southern Seminoles were faced with forced resettlement to west of the Mississippi River. Angered at having to give up their land, some members of the tribe resisted and moved deep into Florida's Everglades, a swampy area replete with sawgrass savannahs, mangroves, hummocks and natural predators. Because the land was unsuitable for domestic stock, the Seminoles relied on fish and game for survival.

The development of the distinctive Seminole patchwork, crafted from ready-made cloth, came about through contact with non-native settlers and their patchwork crafts, and was furthered through the introduction of hand-cranked sewing machines. To this day, Seminole men and women fashion and wear their distinctive patchwork shirts, jackets, capes, aprons, and skirts. The geometric Seminole patterns are made of small elements, arranged in continuous and varied patterns. Their intense color combinations are reminiscent of the bright colors of beads.

SOCIAL SCIENCE EXPERIENCE

Concept:

When two different cultures come in contact, several results are possible; one possibility is that one culture will provide new raw materials and technology for use by the other.

Objective:

To identify and consider the various results that can come from two different cultures coming in contact with each other.

Activities:

Find newspaper stories about today's Seminole bingo games and other facets of their economy. Compare these to the Seminole lifestyle of the past.

Research the traditional Seminole lifestyle and geographic area pre-1800's.

Discuss why the Seminoles treasure their traditional ways and which customs they retain from their past.

Compare the Seminoles to other native American people.

ART EXPERIENCE

Concept:

Repetition of shape and color unifies design.

Objectives:

To experiment with patchwork design.

To create a design using the repetition of simple units.

To combine individual designs into patterns using alternation, reversal and angular placement for cutting.

Activity:

Materials: Fadeless paper (4 colors), manila paper, scissors, paste, a ruler, a pencil.

Directions: Cut four 1" x 18" strips of paper and paste them side by side (touching) on the manila paper. Cut the pasted strips crosswise in 1" wide strips. Place these strips of cut squares on the manila sheet so that the corners of the squares meet and form a checkerboard pattern. Experiment with cutting the original strips at 45° and 60° angles, also with different arrangements of colors and widths or positions. Paste a group on a poster board to form a pattern for a piece of patchwork fabric to be made into an apron.

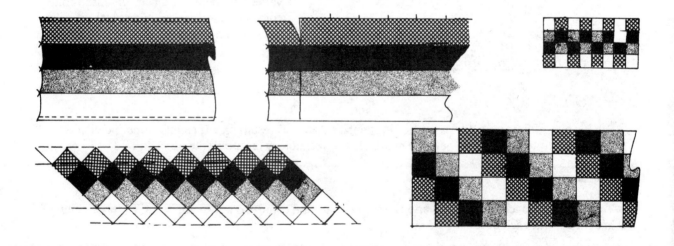

51.   NATIVE AMERICAN SHELL INLAY (C)

Native Americans in both North and South America have valued the pearly iridescence of abalone shells from Pacific ocean waters. The shells were used in ceremonies and as wampum for intertribal trade, as well as for decorative inlays in woodwork, weapons and housekeeping tools. Abalone was traded from tribe to tribe, all over the continent. The most perfect shells were fashioned into decorations, such as pendants and nosepieces. The rest were worked by grinding, shaping and drilling. Often, broken pieces were used as inlays in embroidery work, to decorate leather and fabric garments. Eventually, traders from other parts of the world brought ready-made mirrors and shiny metals which were sub-stituted for the less accessible abalone shells.

Inlay embroiderers fashion "pockets" of thread to hold the shell pieces securely in place, and then stitch compact frames to surround them. Shell inlays may form the center of a design or they may be used to add texture to a repeated pattern.

SOCIAL SCIENCE EXPERIENCE

Concept:

Craftspeople often employ new, more efficient or less expensive techniques and materials to create similar yet different craft items.

Objective:

To identify the reasons why cultures value items; to consider and identify why different cultures value different items.

Activities:

Learn about abalone and their shells; their use as food and as decoration.

Prepare a meal in which abalone is the main ingredient.

Find other items which were traded cross-continent by intertribal commerce.   Describe their uses (Catlinite - pipestone).

ART EXPERIENCE

Concept:

Contrast in texture adds emphasis and variety to a design.

Objectives:

To make a fabric patch with a design of embroidered inlay.

To contrast the textures of inlay and fabric.

To repeat shapes to unify a design.

To exercise needlework and cutting skills.

Activity:

Materials: Yarn, aluminum cans, a needle and thread, a thimble, scissors, chalk, heavy fabric, glue.

Directions: Draw a design on paper and transfer it to fabric. Cut shapes from aluminum cans. Glue the inlays (aluminum shapes) into position (onto the fabric) to them hold while sewing. Stitch (as shown in diagram). When completed, a fabric backing can be sewn over or ironed on, to cover the stitch ends.

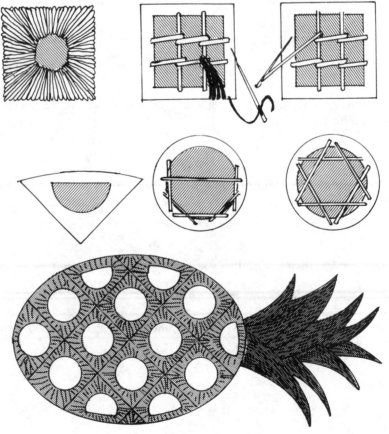

6

CRAFT, ASSEMBLE AND CONSTRUCT

52. AFRICAN ENCRUSTED SCULPTURE (A)

In some African cultures, wood sculptors carve their works from large tree branches or entire logs. Some of the resulting sculptures have highly polished surfaces, while others are heavily encrusted with beads, shells or teeth which have been inset to follow the contours of the piece.

Perhaps the most distinctive encrusted sculpture is produced in Cameroon, on the Gulf of Guinea in west central Africa. From portrait heads to life-sized figures, from tables to calabash utensils, Cameroon decorative objects are covered with shells, teeth and beads.

One important example of encrusted sculpture is the chief religious statue of the Kom people of Cameroon. Called Afo-a-Kom, the century-old statue depicts a man holding a scepter. His face is copper, and his hands and feet are undecorated "iroko" wood. The rest of the life-sized figure (it is a full 5' 2" tall) is covered with bugle-type beads and cowrie shells.

SOCIAL SCIENCE EXPERIENCE

Concept:

The value of art and craft objects is determined by many criteria: the base worth of their materials; the amount of time, skill and labor involved in their creation; their rarity; their aesthetic quality; and their symbolic meaning within their culture.

Objective:

To distinguish between the value of an art or craft object within its culture and its value outside of its culture.

Activities:

Discuss why and how an object made of wood and shells might have great value to a culture beyond the worth of its materials.

List examples of objects in students' own culture that may be similarly valued, though they are made from humble materials (historic artifacts such as: the Liberty Bell, George Washington's false teeth, a photograph of great-grandparents).

Study African encrusted sculpture.

List other objects that are valued for elaborate decoration with humble materials: Mardi Gras costumes of New Orleans, architecture of Antonio Gaudi, clothing of British "Pearlies."

ART EXPERIENCE

Concept:

Changes in texture or color add emphasis to a form.

Objectives:

To make a statue of a figure and accentuate its shape with textured decoration.

To simplify the form of a figure.

To harmonize textures with form.

To develop skills in subtractive sculpture, textural patterning and gluing.

Activity:

Materials: A styrofoam block (8" x 2" x 2"), plastic knives with serrated edges, a base for the figure, beads, buttons, shells, assorted pasta, beans or seeds, glue, paint.

Directions: Use plastic knives to carve a statue of a figure from styrofoam.   Paint its face, hands and feet.   Glue the statue to the base block and let it dry.   Arrange and glue small decorative items to follow the form of the figure.   Cover all of the unpainted surfaces.   Accentuate the round shapes, such as the head, with items glued in concentric circles.   Arrange items in parallel lines to define linear shapes, such as arm lengths.

53. NAMBA HEADMASKS OF VANUATU (A)

The Namba tribespeople live in Vanuatu, formerly known as the New Hebrides Islands, in Melanesia, south of New Guinea.   Like other Melanesians, the Nambas are noted for their seamanship.   Once far-reaching explorers, the Nambas today do not venture too far from their remote part of the Pacific.   However, they still do actively participate in other parts of their cultural traditions.

During ceremonial dances and tribal rituals, the Namba tribesmen, as did their ancestors before them, wear knee-length fiber cloaks and awesome masks which cover their heads and shoulders. Namba maskmakers are specialists, noted for their ability to reproduce traditional designs.   They fashion colorful demons and gods, using materials gathered from their environment, such as shark's skin, coral, bamboo, stones, shells, bones and teeth.   There are "good" masks and "bad" masks, with each appropriately decorated to look either pleasant or fearsome. Protuberances and moving parts are fastened to the masks to make them especially impressive. As their wearers dance, long wands with feathery attachments, flowers, woven straw or leaves jiggle about and serve to animate the features of the masks.

SOCIAL SCIENCE EXPERIENCE

Concept:

Artifacts such as masks are symbolic representations of such concepts as demons and gods. Masks are both symbols and objects.

Objective:

To recognize both the tangible reality and the intangible symbolism embodied in certain objects.

Activities:

Consider the tangible reality of currency such as the United States' dollar.   Likewise, consider the dollar's symbolic attributes.

Consider the tangible reality of a postage stamp.   Likewise, consider the stamp's symbolic attributes.

List the objects considered by students to possess the most symbolical status. Also, list the objects most coveted by students. Compare the lists; explore the reasons for the students' having invested status and power in an object; explore their motives for wanting to possess an object.

ART EXPERIENCE

Concept:

Natural forms can be simplified or abstracted to the point of becoming geometric shapes.

Objectives:

To make a head mask.

To simplify the facial features into geometric shapes: spheres, tubes, discs, and others.

To use contrasting colors to make patterns on the face.

To emphasize the dominant feature by using distortion, color contrast or movement.

To gain skill in constructing and painting.

Activity:

Materials: newspaper, cardboard, paste, clay, large balloons, a nail, string, balsa wood, feathers, flowers, tempera paints, broom straws, cardboard tubes, and so on.

Directions: Use the balloon as a mold for forming a papier mache' head covering. Cover the enlarged balloon with wet strips of paper, and then with three layers of pasted strips. Using pasted paper strips, attach rolls of cardboard or other items (for making the shapes of eyes, nose, ear, chin, and other features). After drying, add flowers, feathers, straws and sticks to the back and sides of the head. Add a cardboard cone on top. Tie strings to the straws. Glue all pieces securely. Let dry. Paint the dried surfaces with details of the features.

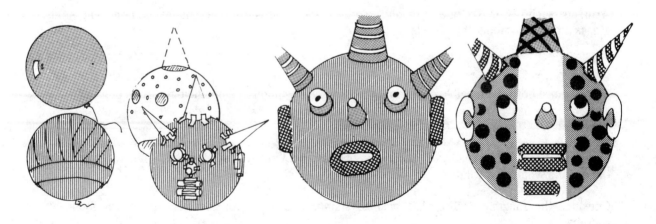

54. INUIT STACKED FIGURES (A)

Scattered throughout north-central Canada are ancient cairns (piles of stones deliberately made by humans) that resemble people wearing heavy winter garb. The theory is offered that the figures were lined up to simulate a row of hunters in order to artificially augment the size of ancient Inuit hunting parties. As herds of caribou were driven past the stone figures, a few real hunters may have hidden behind the stones and shouted to frighten the herd, causing the animals to hasten forward to their doom at the hands of the rest of the hunting party.

The people who made the stacked figures carefully selected the stones to be used. None of the stones were cut or chipped to fit. The blocks were both large and heavy. The stones were matched to each other so well that generations of winter storms have not tumbled them.

SOCIAL SCIENCE EXPERIENCE

Concept:

Strategy and tactics are as important to hunters as strength and weaponry.

Objective:

To recognize and compare the different qualities that can yield power: strength, intelligence and others.

Activities:

Identify other uses of figures or objects to "fool" animals (decoys, bullfighter's cape).

Explain how hunting skills are employed in today's culture.

Play a game involving strategy and tactics.

Search newspapers and magazines for examples of the use of strategy and tactics in business or in sporting events.

Find evidence of clever strategies that resulted in success for warriors, politicians, cartoon characters, characters in literature and others.

Relate personal anecdotes about applied cleverness.

ART EXPERIENCE

Concept:

Symmetrical balance has the weight, size and number of items evenly distributed on both sides of a center line or point.

Objectives:

To make a figure of stacked stones.

To achieve the balance of the stones without depending on glue.

To increase skills in fitting and construction.

Activity:

Materials: 4 rocks (large and flat), at least 16 more rocks (that are similar in size to the first 4), clear adhesive, a wooden base.

Directions: Glue the "foot" rocks, slightly separated, to the base. (As stones are added, be sure they will balance and fit before gluing.) Add "leg" stones and a bridging "hip" stone, and glue them all together. Leave them until they are dry. Next, add "body" stones, "arms" (long flat stones, added under the shoulder stone if desired), shoulder stone, neck and head. Glue each stone into place. Statues may be lined up in a diorama. (Use quilt batting or sand for snow. Include toy deer and men.)

55. JEWELED EGGS OF RUSSIA (A)

There are two kinds of highly decorated Easter eggs on display in museums and private collections in the U.S.S.R. and around the world. One consists of intricately decorated chicken eggshells, called "psanky" (see Lesson 48) which are crafted by Ukrainians and people in other eastern European cultures. The other kind of eggs, more rare and much more costly, are actually egg-shaped, jeweled and enameled masterpieces, designed by the goldsmith, Carl Faberge', a jeweler who created these and other ornaments for the czars who ruled Russia in the late 19th century.

Altogether, the artisans in the Faberge' workshop made only fifty-eight eggs which were commissioned by the imperial family to exchange as gifts, just as simpler folk exchanged psanky eggs.

The fabulous Faberge' creations were made of gold, silver, platinum, enamel and gems. On the outside of each were such decorations as portraits of the royal family, clocks, ornaments and jewels. Inside each egg was a remarkable three-dimensional surprise, such as a mechanical songbird, a miniature palace, a tiny basket of jeweled flowers or a replica of a royal coach.

After the Russian Revolution, many of these treasures became the property of the Russian State. Today, many Faberge' eggs are displayed in the armory of the Kremlin in Moscow, a museum of Russian cultural heritage.

SOCIAL SCIENCE EXPERIENCE

Concept:

Simple symbols with religious, seasonal and other meanings can be transformed into symbols of power and prestige.

Objective:

To identify the types of objects that are meant to convey an impression of power.

Activities:

List examples of the wealthy and powerful people imitating humble crafts with expensive materials: Faberge' eggs, Yves St. Laurent's "peasant" fashions, Marie Antoinette's "gardener's cottage," yuppy stone-washed denims. Consider why these expensive copies of simple things represent wealth. Discuss the reasoning, motives and values behind the adoption of these items.

Find pictures of expensive, power objects and their "humble" counterparts: castles/gingerbread castles, furs/fake-fur jackets, diamond jewelry/rhinestone jewelry.   Make an exhibit of your comparisons.

Study the life, period and creations of Carl Faberge'.

ART EXPERIENCE

Concept:

Repetition unifies design.   The use of unusual or surprising materials can add emphasis, variety and visual interest to a design.

Objectives:

To create a jeweled egg with a portrait or a photograph as its centerpiece, to give as a gift.

To emphasize the portrait by framing.

To lend unity to the piece with repetition of color, shape, decorative motif.

To gain skill in gluing and cutting.

Activity:

Materials: A portrait or photograph (of a person, idol or pet), de'coupage trims, old costume jewelry, sequins, metallic braiding, rhinestones, glue, medium-to-dark-colored enamel spray paint, an egg-shaped hosiery container.

Directions: If desired, spray paint the egg-shaped container a deeper color.   Trim the portrait to a vertical oval, 1 1/2" x 1 1/4".   Glue the egg-shaped container halves together.   Next, holding the egg pointed end up, glue the portrait to the center of the egg.   Trim around the border of the portrait with glued on sequins or rhinestones.   Also, glue rows of trim around the egg.   Embellish the egg further with "jewels" and sequins.   Make a stand for the egg to sit on.

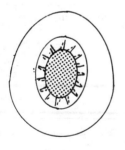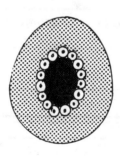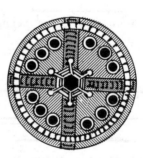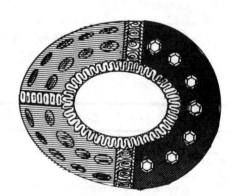

56. HAMAMATSU FIGHTING KITES (B)

The people of Japan have many customs and celebrations that involve the flying of kites. Likewise, Japanese stories tell of clever thieves or escaping heroes who are carried aloft by kites. So popular are kites that the cities and regions of Japan hold annual kite-flying festivals in which certain traditional kite shapes have become identified with particular areas. Kites from Niigata are hexagonal, for example, while those from Matsue, Ehime and Tsugaru are rectangular. Kagura kites resemble lanterns, Tokushima kites are mandala-shaped, and Nagasaki kites are diamond-shaped with tassels. In other districts, kites are shaped as fish, people or geometric figures such as the letter "T."

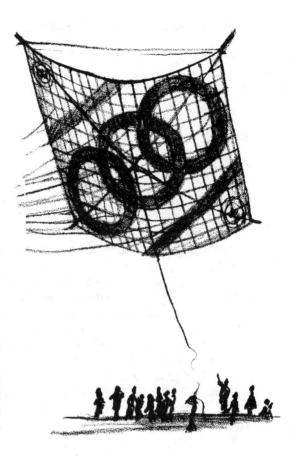

Whatever their basic shapes, kites may be decorated with scenic pictures, famous characters or symmetrical line designs. A favorite decoration, a samurai warrior in armor and helmet, is used on kites flown on boys' day, a national holiday.

The people of Hamamatsu hold a yearly festival in which "birthday kites" compete. Groups of parents whose sons have reached their first birthday band together in teams to build huge kites which are flown in "kite-fights." The objective is to try to knock the other kites out of the sky. The last kite left flying is the winner and the sons of that team's members will have good luck.

SOCIAL SCIENCE EXPERIENCE

Concept:

Regions and cities become known for special symbols and particular craft products.

Objective:

To identify particular objects that are visual symbols of particular places.

Activities:

List some visual symbols and the regions that they represent.

List traditional crafts that are associated with birthday celebrations, coming of age ceremonies, weddings, and other rites of passage.

Collect patches or pins showing the symbols of cities, states and regions.

ART EXPERIENCE

Concept:

Design should fit the shape of the format.

Objectives:

To make a kite and decorate it with a symbolic design.

To simplify detail giving the kite's decoration a uniqueness that can be identified even at a distance.

To increase construction and painting skills.

Activity:

Materials: Tissue paper, paste, string, watercolors, brushes, a ruler, 5 (3' x 1/2" x 1/16") lengths of bamboo (balsa or basswood), a knife, scissors.

Directions: Sketch a design, then carefully draw and paint it at the center of a 16" square of tissue paper. Leave a margin of two inches or more all around the outer edges of the design. Cut two (14") and two (16") sticks. Place the 14" sticks at opposite edges on the back of the paper. Fold a 1" flap of paper over each stick, then paste the flaps over the sticks. Place a 16" stick at the top edge and another at the bottom edge of the paper. Fold over 1" flaps and paste them over the sticks. Lay the two remaining sticks diagonally on the back of the paper. Cut them to include the diagonal length plus 1" (to extend 1/2" beyond the corners of the kite). Staple (or tie) the diagonal sticks to the top and bottom sticks. Cut a 16" stick. Lay it horizontally, halfway between the top and bottom sticks. Where the horizontal stick crosses the vertical sticks, carefully pierce the tissue (with a pencil point) and tie the crossing sticks together. To string the kite, tie a length of string to each end of the horizontal center stick. Pull the string taut until the kite bows. Next, turn the kite over and attach strings to each of the five points. Carefully pierce the tissue and tie the strings to the kite's stick frame. Gather the ends of all five strings and securely tie them to a flying string (hundreds of feet long). Try adding paper tails to the bottom corners of the kite. Make them each twice as long as the kite itself.

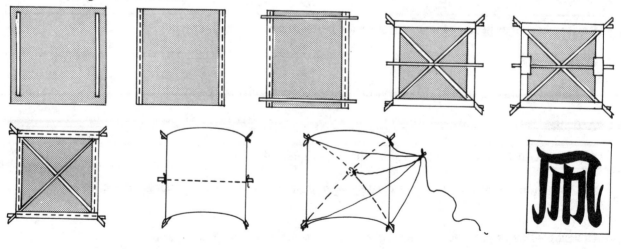

57. DARK MASKS AND THE THIRD EYE (B)

Throughout history many cultures have accepted new beliefs and customs without discarding their old ones. While the ancient Egyptians simply added new deities to their roster until they had collected some 400 gods, the Romans matched Greek gods with Roman deities, and adapted elements from both Egyptian and Middle Eastern cults to their religious beliefs.

In modern Mexico, ancient Aztec and Christian celebrations have been combined. While in the West Indies, elements of Christianity are mixed with African religious beliefs. In the United States, today, Halloween, a Christian holiday with pagan overtones, is celebrated by most people as a completely secular holiday.

The people of Ladakh, an area of northern India between Kashmir and Tibet, have modified Buddhism into Lamaism, and produced their own local variation. They believe that Lama tamed a thousand demons and made them the guardians of Buddhism. In an annual celebration, the people of Ladakh wear demon masks and re-enact Lama's great feat. The grotesque demon heads are fitted over the shoulders of dancers who are dressed in plain saffron robes. Their fierce masks have three fiery eyes, glowering expressions, and bared teeth.

SOCIAL SCIENCE EXPERIENCE

Concept:

Cultures may adopt new ideas or combine them with their old ideas.

Objective:

To discover the origins of holiday symbols.

Activities:

Describe religious and secular symbols in holidays.

List old ideas in our culture that exist concurrently with new ones: herbal remedies with modern medicines, the "Man in the Moon" and men on the moon, the "lucky rabbit's foot" that has become the "lucky penny."

Study the use of masks in various religions and cultures. Create a mask for a personal holiday or event.

Make an exhibit of "old" and "new" ideas that are concurrently held in our culture.

ART EXPERIENCE

Concept:

Distortion (miniaturization, exaggeration) focuses attention and adds emphasis to an image.

Objectives:

To construct a "whole head" mask that shows a violent emotion.

To distort features to emphasize the theme.

To show contrast in value, texture and color.

To enhance skills in forming and painting.

Activity:

Materials: A round balloon, papier mache', a bowl, glue, scissors, paint, brushes, 2 yards of cheese cloth.

Directions: Inflate the balloon larger than the head size of the person who will wear the mask.   Cover the balloon with three to five layers of papier mache' strips and let dry.   Trim the back and bottom of the papier mache' form to fit over the head and neck, and rest it on the shoulders of its wearer.   Remove.   Next, mix finely-chopped papier mache' into the consistency of dough and apply to the head mask to make eyes (three, if desired.)   Then, shape the eyebrows and ears, the nose, cheeks, mouth, teeth, tongue and beard.   Paint, when dry, and drape the mask with strings of cheese cloth for hair.

   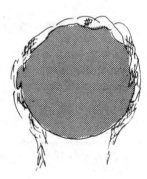

58. JADE FANS OF KATMANDU (B)

Nepal is one of the world's most remote kingdoms. Its capital, Katmandu, shimmers with the mystery of the East and has changed little over the centuries. In recent times, during ceremonial outings, the king of Nepal has continued to ride about in a gilt-covered "howda" (saddle basket) atop a royal elephant.

The skill of the Nepalese craftworkers in gold, silver, copper, bronze and other materials accounts for Nepal's rich heritage in the arts. Among the most splendid treasures displayed in Nepalese pageants are their jade and peacock feather fans. Shaped like teardrops, the fans have photographs of honored persons in their centers, which are surrounded by jade discs and borders of peacock feathers.

SOCIAL SCIENCE EXPERIENCE

Concept:

Geographic isolation can slow change in a culture.

Objectives:

Locate Nepal on a map and identify the geographic features that isolate the country from its neighbors.

Consider the recent changes that have made Nepal less isolated.

Note an element in the description of the jade fans that indicates there has been a recent change in their construction (i.e., photography has replaced painted portraits).

Activities:

Select a few modern technologies (photography, electricity, satellites, lasers) and study how they have (or haven't infiltrated isolated cultures.

ART EXPERIENCE

Concept:

Outlining and framing add emphasis to an image.

Activities:

Make a fan with a framed portrait in the center.

Emphasize and "glorify" the portrait with elaborate framing.

Gain unity by repeating shapes and colors.

Add movement with feather trim.

Increase skill in cutting, constructing and painting.

Materials: Poster board, feathers, metallic paper; photograph, painted portrait or portrait cut from a magazine; scissors, glue, staples, metallic spray, paper doilies.

Directions: From poster board, cut out 2 tear drops 10" at bottom by 15" high, and 8 circles 3" in diameter. Cut the photo (or portrait) into a vertical oval approximately 4" x 5". Spray the doilies with metallic paint. Place the photograph in the center of one teardrop and ring it with 3" discs. With glue, draw a border around the photo and apply trim cut from the doilies. Glue a 1" circle of metallic paper in the centers of the discs. Apply trim around the discs (to match the center's trim). Edge the back of the teardrop with feathers. Use staples to hold them securely in place. Lay the front teardrop over the back teardrop and staple them together (with the feathers between). Insert a triangular, folded posterboard handle at the bottom of the fan (between the front and back teardrops) and secure it with staples and glue.

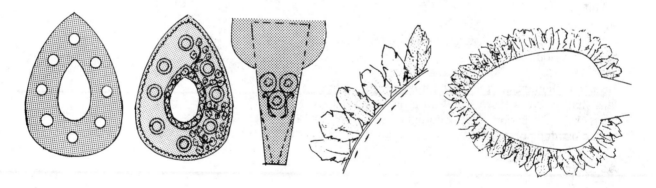

59. CARNIVAL COSTUMES OF TRINIDAD (B)

Carnival in colonial Trinidad originated as an imitation of the elegant "masques" (masked balls) held in France and the rest of Europe. Each year Trinidad's French settlers celebrated the last day before the start of the Christian observance of Lent by dressing in colorful masks and festive costumes, then marching in a grand parade and attending glittering balls.

In more recent times, the annual Carnival parade has been adopted and updated by Trinidad's current citizens who are, for the most part, the descendants of the island's native Indians, former slaves from Africa, and/or European settlers. Gaiety is the keynote of Carnival, and its costumes have grown increasingly lavish.

Unlike the original French imports, Carnival costumes of today are locally made, using all kinds of available materials. The extravagant costumes and elaborate parade floats glitter with tinsel, cellophane, sequins, paper flowers, oilcloth ornaments, and metallic dust. Many Carnival costumes are accentuated with giant headdresses, so large, that to prevent their collapse, they must be carefully balanced and supported by wires, as the marchers bob and weave through the parade.

SOCIAL SCIENCE EXPERIENCE

Concept:

Customs may change as they are adopted by another culture.

Objective:

To recognize the reasons why one culture would adopt the custom(s) or behaviors of another; likewise to consider the results, positive or negative, that might occur.

Activities:

Study European masked balls and carnival parades in Rio de Janeiro, New Orleans, and Trinidad.

Work as a group to make costumed figures for a carnival parade.

Discuss the reasons why people participate in carnivals (and other festival-like activities).

Participate in a local festival. Keep a log of activities, personal benefits and problems. Share the highlights of the experience by writing a newspaper article about it.

ART EXPERIENCE

Concept:

Unity is a harmonious relationship, a oneness between subject, materials and the presentation of a product (art or other).

Objectives:

To make a Carnival costume on a papier mache' figure.

To develop unity between the theme of the costume and its colors and materials.

To gain skill in pattern-making, sewing, and the forming of figures.

Activity:

Materials: A wooden block (the base), 2 wire hangers, cloth, sequins, braiding, string, foil, glitter, spangles, and other decorations, glue, needles, thread, scissors, tape, a hammer, nails, papier mache', paint.

Directions: Select a theme for a Carnival parade (Spring, a historical period, a quotation) and collect the materials needed to make costumed figures. Using wire, form the core of a figure in action and anchor the armature to a wooden block base. Paint the base, if desired. Cover the figure with papier mache' and tape it (as shown in the diagram). Clothe the figure, first cutting and fitting paper patterns before cutting the cloth. Allow 1/4" to 1/2" edge margins in the paper patterns (for hems and seams). Fabricate an elaborate headdress and cover the headdress and costume with beads, spangles, braiding and other items. (Several figures will make a lively parade.)

60. KOREAN FOLK MINIATURES (C)

Miniatures are different from dolls in that they are not intended to be handled as play-things. Usually miniatures are fragile and very detailed. Also, unlike many dolls, miniatures have no moveable parts.

Korean folk miniatures are noted for their characteristic dress and gestures. The adult figures are 8" to 12" high and all have exaggerated heads and facial features. They are genre figures, posed as if in the midst of the activities of daily life, such as carrying children, baskets, chickens, food or tools. Miniatures are usually displayed on wooden blocks and are constructed of papier mache' formed over a wire frame. Facial features, including hair, are painted on the papier mache' forms. Then clothing and appropriate small-scale artifacts are added to complete the characterization.

SOCIAL SCIENCE EXPERIENCE

Concept:

Miniatures can represent the character and role types of a culture.

Objectives:

To identify the similarities and differences between miniatures, dolls and models, especially in terms of what each represents in a culture.

Activities:

List various types of miniatures that also can be used as toys (British lead soldiers, model trains, doll house furniture).

Distinguish these toys from those miniatures that are intended for other purposes (Kachina dolls, ships in bottles, historical reproduction rooms, porcelain figurines, architectural models, nativity figures).

Discuss the concept of caricature and use; apply it to describe the appropriate props for various occupations.

Locate a miniature-maker in your town or city (a model-maker, architectural designer, doll house furniture maker). Invite him or her to speak to your class.

Draw caricatures of people with whom you are acquainted, such as: teachers, politicians, parents, bus/cab/truck drivers, and others.

ART EXPERIENCE

Concepts:

Gesture imparts movement to a figure.

Distortion (miniaturization or other exaggeration) adds emphasis to the character of an image.

Objectives:

To make a genre caricature of a person from everyday life (not a particular individual).

To develop physical balance in a three-dimensional figure.

To create movement through depicting a gesture.

To build a form on an armature.

To make a pattern.

To increase skills in tying, painting, sewing.

Activity:

Materials: Six feet of soft wire, newspaper, white tissue paper, tape, paste, a wooden block, a hammer, nails, pliers, brushes, white glue, string, cloth for a costume.

Directions: Build a head, body and legs armature with soft wire.   Add arms.   Position the figure as if in action: walking, working, playing.   Secure the feet to the wooden block with nails.   Tape the twisted wires firmly.   Wrap the figure with dampened newspaper, either in flat strips or well-squeezed mush.   Flesh out the figure.   Wind string around the figure to securely hold the newspaper in place.   Cover with 1" strips of pasted newspaper, then cover with smooth white tissue paper.   Let the figure dry.   Paint the face and figure, before dressing it. Design a costume to show its occupation, nationality or historical period.   Make tissue paper patterns of the garments and fit the patterns before cutting the cloth.   Leave 1/4" around the pattern pieces for seams and for hem. Glue or sew the garments in place.

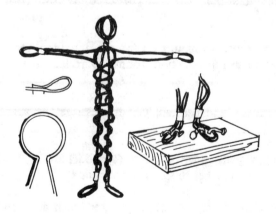

61. SPIRIT MASKS OF NEW GUINEA (C)

In New Guinea, traditions are transferred orally and through songs, stories and rituals. The tribesmen of New Guinea have a "spirit cult" which passes from one generation of males to the next in a ceremonial initiation rite stressing bravery.

During the initiation, the men of the tribe, wearing masks, charge out from their ceremonial building and chase away the adolescent boys, women and children, scaring everybody. The masks represent the spirits of local heroes who, when alive, were inspirations to the tribe. The adolescent boy initiates must find the courage and the cunning to enter the ceremonial building, in spite of the frightening behavior of the men who are challenging them. By passing this test, the boys show that they are worthy of becoming men in the tribe.

SOCIAL SCIENCE EXPERIENCE

Concept:

Cultures value unique standards of personal behavior. Each one equates the presence (or absence) of these characteristics with a person's potential for success.

Objective:

To identify the categories of behavioral characteristics that are valued at different developmental levels of societies (compare those valued in primitive societies with those valued in industrialized societies); to find similarities and dissimilarities.

Activities:

Discuss the importance of courage to a tribesman in New Guinea.

Identify the qualities that bring success in business, sports, politics, the arts, society and the professions. Select individuals who are well-known in each field. Discover the personal qualities in each that led to his/her success.

Recognize the role of gender in the formation of learned personal qualities that are encouraged by different societies.

Identify the personal characteristics valued most by students themselves, by their parents, and by their friends. Write essays about how these values were/are/can be developed.

ART EXPERIENCE

Concept:

Design can be based on the imitation, exaggeration or simplification of nature.

Objectives:

To make a mask using a simple one-piece press mold.

To simplify the facial contours and exaggerate the size of the features by enlarging the eyes and reducing the nose and mouth.

To gain skill in forming (sculpting).

Activity:

Materials: Clay, plaster of Paris, papier mache', a tape measure, a board (2' x 3'), a bowl, a bucket, tempera paints, talcum powder, clear plastic spray, scrap linoleum strips (3" or more by 3' or more), thin cloth.

Directions: Measure the real face that the mask will cover. Mark the dimensions on the plywood board and mound the clay to the shape and depth of the face. Design a mask with a dominant (exaggerated) feature. Add clay to give the mask an elongated shape. Smooth the surfaces. Make the eyes very prominent. Finish the modeling of features. Place the linoleum strip around the outside of the mask (to contain the liquid plaster when it is poured), and anchor the strip to the table with clay. Mix the plaster to a heavy cream consistency. Pour the plaster over the clay to cover the highest point with 1/2" of plaster. Let the plaster set and then clean out the clay. Dry the plaster mold for a week. Seal the mold with several coats of plastic spray. Then, dust it with talcum powder. Mix papier mache' into a soft pulp in a mixer and apply to the underside of the mold, pressing into the indentations and keeping an even thickness of 1/4". While the mache' is still wet, add thick cloth strips to the inside for added strength. Let the mache' dry completely, remove the mask from the mold, and then paint.

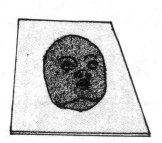 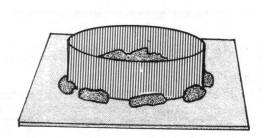 

62. RUSSIAN BUTTERFLY WINDOWS (C)

The Volga and the Ob rivers are the "highways" of the great plains of central Russia. Their tributaries link villages, towns and cities, transporting not only goods, but arts and culture, as well.

Historically, the buildings in many river towns and villages have been built of wood in a simple design and then adorned with fancy woodwork carefully executed by skilled craftsmen. In Tobolsk, on a tributary of the Ob, visitors can admire beautifully carved window frames featuring multiple layers of delicate scrollwork. Likewise, on the Volga, the windows of the village homes are decorated with intricately carved panels.

The traditional Russian woodworkers created a unique style of cut and pierced designs, which were layered to produce a relief effect. Mechanical tools helped to make the work on the frames progress more quickly and precisely. Looking like beautiful butterflies, the completed windows display an infinite variety of skillful artistry.

Unfortunately, there is little or no call for the traditional woodwork designs on the new, modern housing units being built today. However, outstanding examples on historic buildings are valued for their beauty and are being preserved.

SOCIAL SCIENCE EXPERIENCE

Concept:

Craft traditions may die unless a conscious effort is made to conserve them.

Objective:

To consider the positive and negative qualities of change; to recognize the features, benefits and drawbacks of progress.

Activities:

Discuss skills and occupations that have been lost due to obsolescence: blacksmithing, baking from scratch, growing one's own food, sewing one's own clothes and others.

List craft skills that people practice today mainly for enjoyment: throwing pottery, knitting, cabinet making and so on.

Study American "gingerbread" house decorations and remark on their similarity to Russian window frames.

Research the role and lifestyle of itinerant craftspeople in Europe and America.

Gather data (photos, measurements, documents) about the different styles of architecture in your community; especially the typical examples and also the unique or unusual designs.

Choose a skill that is becoming obsolete and learn it.

ART EXPERIENCE

Concept:

Layers, sculpted and arranged in relief, suggest spatial depth.

Objectives:

To make a layered wooden frame.

To create harmony in design by using a repeated motif.

To develop depth by overlapping layers.

To design the top piece as dominant and the lower ones as subordinate in motif.

To gain skill using drill and saw, constructing and painting.

Activity:

Materials: Five 3' strips of balsa wood (measuring 1/4" x 2", 1/4" x 1/4", 1/8" x 1", 1/8" x 2", and 1/8" x 3"), an X-Acto knife, a coping saw, nails, glue, a drill and bits, paint.

Directions: Cut the 1/4" x 2" strip into two pieces 10" long and two pieces 8" long.   Make a frame by gluing the ends of the 8" pieces to the inside sides (left and right) of the 10" pieces. The inside measurements should be 6" x 8".   Cut the 1/4" x 1/4" strip into two 8" and two 5 1/2" lengths.   Then place the pieces on top of the inner edge of the frame and glue them in place.   Plan a design to modify the square corners with curves.   Build up the outer edges of the frame with the 1" and 2" wide strips.   Next, drill or punch holes in the pieces to form a pattern.   Use a coping saw to cut curves and other shapes.   Fit all of the pieces before gluing them together.   Use two colors to paint the contrasting elements in the frame.   Use as a picture frame.

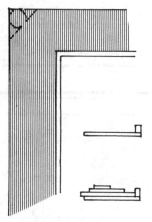

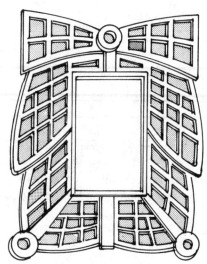

7

PAINT, ILLUSTRATE AND DECORATE

63. ENGLISH SIGNS THAT "SHOW AND TELL" (A)

Today, the inns and pubs of Great Britain are colorful landmarks, readily identified by distinctive signs which hang over their doors. Most of the signs continue to display both pictorial symbols and spelled-out names, a practice that has persisted from the days when many people could not read.

The pictures and names on the signs are practical, varied, and sometimes, fanciful. Most are derived from geographic landmarks, historic events, common occupations, famous people or symbolic animals. For example, more than one tavern in Berkshire is called "The White Horse," after a locally famous landmark, the White Horse of Uffington, a huge horse sculpture, made of natural chalk, cut from under the turf of a nearby hillside. Signs identifying the inns all picture a large white horse.

Other examples of pub names are: "The King George," with a profile of a man's head (meant to represent the king), "The Hare and Hound," with a picture of a hound in hot pursuit of a hare, and "The Crown and Anchor," with pictures of each.

SOCIAL SCIENCE EXPERIENCE

Concept:

Communication is both visual and verbal.

Objective:

To examine the qualities, both capabilities and limitations, associated with various communication modes.

Activities:

Discuss the role of the inn, tavern or pub as a central gathering place in English culture.

Evaluate the effectiveness of simple words and shapes on signs viewed from a moving vehicle; consider the international highway signs and other travel symbols advocated by the United Nations.

Share ideas as to important events, people or places that would make good names for a club or gathering place.

Study English inn and pub signs. Design a sign for your own group or clubhouse.

Cut out examples of effective signs that use pictures to parallel their language. Explain why they have impact.

Cut out pictures or logos you might not understand if you could not read: "Texaco," for example, might be "Star Gas."

ART EXPERIENCE

Concept:

Simplified shapes or images can lend impact to a design.

Objectives:

To design a sign for display.

To integrate words and pictures into a unified message.

To simplify an image for rapid reading.

To increase drawing and lettering skills and introduce flat brush lettering.

Activity:

Materials: Mat board, tempera (or acrylic) paints, a flat brush, a round brush, a hole punch.

Directions: Decide on a name. Then, make several small sketches for a sign to display the name; be sure the words and pictures match. Paint the sign with strong color contrasts, using the flat brush for one-stroke lettering. The sign may be painted on both sides, and the outline shaped if desired. Punch holes to hang the sign.

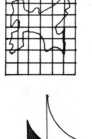
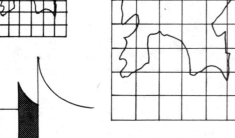

64. PAPER BLOSSOMS OF JAPAN (A)

"While bad luck seems able to find its way into daily life on its own, good luck needs guidance!"

Many westerners depend on wishing wells, birthday candles, rabbits' feet, favorite numbers, four leaf clovers or other lucky charms to bring them good fortune. Similarly, the Japanese practice many customs that they believe may help to "tilt the odds" in their favor.

When visiting the Shinto shrine at Heian, Japanese pilgrims buy good luck fortunes written on durable rice paper. They are much larger than those found in Chinese restaurant fortune cookies.

The actual writing is done by skilled calligraphers, writing specialists, who use brushes and ink to create the messages on the paper. The writing consists of a series of elegant pictographs. Each pictograph represents a word or an idea. When combined, the pictographs produce the more complex thoughts expressed in the fortunes.

The Japanese people use lengths of string to fasten the fortunes to the branches of the trees that stand in front of the shrine. Unrolled and fluttering loosely in the breeze, like white blossoms in the sun, each paper represents someone's expectation of good luck.

SOCIAL SCIENCE EXPERIENCE

Concept:

Many cultures recognize chance or luck as a factor in the fortunes of people.

Objective:

To compare the philosophical notions of luck as destiny with the personal control of events.

Activities:

List examples of how people try to affect their "luck." Include examples of activities sure to produce bad luck: walking under ladders, crossing paths with black cats, stepping on cracks and more.

Examine the differences between luck and opportunity. Read about real and imaginary characters who have been dubbed "Lucky" and discuss how "lucky" they really were: "Lucky Lindy," "Lucky Jim," and "Lucky Luciano."

ART EXPERIENCE

Concept:

The character of a line is determined by the tool and medium used to draw it, and the surface to which it is applied.

Objectives:

To construct a "good luck" tree.

To gain fluency in brush lettering.

To develop contrast in line thickness.

Activity:

Materials: A pot filled with stones, a bare tree branch, a pointed watercolor brush, black and red inks, black thread, white tissue paper, plaster of Paris.

Directions: Use stones to firmly anchor the branch in the pot. Fill the pot with plaster of Paris. Cut the tissue into 1 1/4" x 7" strips. Copy one or two of the Japanese good luck pictographs or design good luck pictographs of your own, such as a smile face or a dollar sign. Paint the pictographs in black on tissue paper strips. Sign your initials in red and use black thread to tie the finished fortune strip to a branch.

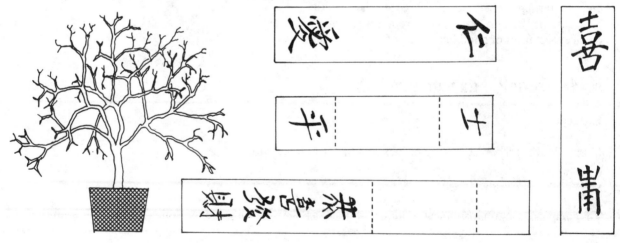

65. MEXICAN TREE PAINTING (A)

Most artists are constantly experimenting with new media or unusual materials. In Mexico, one such experiment has proved to be beneficial to painters and to trees, the unusual material on which the painters paint. Besides receiving fees for their efforts, the Mexican tree painters get to enjoy the challenge of decorating oddly-shaped and rough-textured "canvases." As for the trees, their appearance is changed forever, and in addition, they are protected from the woodboring insects that otherwise might kill them.

Mexican shopkeepers hire artists to paint signs on the trees that stand in front of their stores. A barber may have spiraling red and white stripes painted on his tree, while other merchants will ask for their trees to be covered with descriptive pictures of their goods or services.

Throughout history, artists have made use of other textured backgrounds (besides trees) to enhance their subject matter. Perhaps the earliest known example is the cave artist who used a protruding rock formation to form the shoulder of a bison he was painting. Likewise, the best Mexican tree painters integrate the natural features of the trees as parts of their designs.

SOCIAL SCIENCE EXPERIENCE

Concept:

Trade depends on public knowledge that a product or service is available.

Objective:

To identify and analyze the steps involved in trade.

Activities:

List different types of advertising media, from word-of-mouth to signs, to billboards, to television commercials. Discuss the role of advertising in contemporary life.

Assume the role of a merchant and decide the best ways to advertise your product or service. Decide how to reach the most potential customers.

Research the real costs of media advertising in your community.

Invite a representative of a local advertising agency to speak to the class about the advertising business.

ART EXPERIENCE

Concept:

Two-dimensional design can be displayed on three-dimensional surfaces.

Objectives:

To paint a tree limb using its natural curves and texture to enhance your design.

To develop painting skills.

Activity:

Materials: A heavy tree limb (diameter at least 2" or 3") with at least one fork, oil or acrylic paints, brushes, solvent, plaster of Paris, a large (5" or more) can or plastic bottle.

Directions: Trim the branches from the tree limb.   Mix plaster in the can (for use as a heavy base to support the limb).   Insert the limb into the damp plaster, then, brace it until the plaster sets.   Sketch the tree branch and try out several designs.   Use the natural features of the branch in the design.   When ready to paint, cover the plaster base with paper (to catch drips), then apply the design.

66.   TUAREG PAINTED LEATHER (A)

The Tuaregs are a nomadic people who range the southern regions of the Sahara Desert. Although Tuareg base camps are relatively stable, the people live in tents (rather than permanent buildings) and move their homes to new locations with the change of seasons. The Tuaregs depend on camels not only for transportation, but also for food. The harshness of their native environment has conditioned the Tuaregs to be reliable pilots for desert caravans as well as to be courageous warriors. While the Taureg men are away from home camp on trading expeditions or directing caravans, those Tuareg women who have servants to care for their homes occupy themselves with decorating leather.

Tuareg leatherwork is both painted and incised. To expand the size or shape of a design, additional pieces of leather are sewn together, as needed. Brilliant patterns combining red, yellow, black, blue and turquoise pieces, executed to contrast with the subtle golds and tans of the leather, are the hallmark of Taureg leatherwork.

SOCIAL SCIENCE EXPERIENCE

Concept:

Cultures with few natural resources create crafts with the materials that are available.

Objective:

To learn about the lifestyle, economy and resources of a nomadic tribe.

Activities:

Gather data on nomadic tribes and their resources, focusing on the Tuaregs.

Discuss how articles of leather might be used in a nomadic household.

Visit the ethnological department of a museum, and identify objects that were used by nomads, and objects that were made from animal hides, hooves, antlers and skins.

Invite a local leatherworker to your class to show samples of different kinds of leather and describe their features, as well as to demonstrate techniques of leatherworking.

ART EXPERIENCE

Concept:

Repetition of motif creates a pattern.

Objectives:

To decorate a leather bag with a repeated motif.

To introduce stamped (impressed) work.

To gain skill in sewing and painting leather.

Activity:

Materials: Chamois skin polishing cloth, leather shoe laces, a hammer, a nail, linen thread, a board, shears, chalk, acrylic paints (in red, yellow, black, blue and/or turquoise), a brush.

Directions: Cut a circle, 3 1/2" in diameter for the bottom of a bag and a sidepiece, 10" x 5". Make a circular design on the bottom in chalk. On the sidepiece, draw a repeating design across 9 1/2", leaving 1/4" on each end for a seam. For the stamped ornamentation, use a nail head or some other metal object to tap indentations along the lines of the design. Carefully paint the leather in the spaces between the stamped lines. Sew the sidepiece to bottom. Overlap the ends of the sidepiece and sew them together.

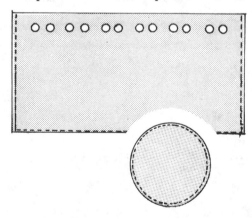 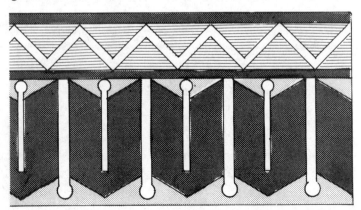

67.   PAINTER WITH A BEAR-HAIR BRUSH (A)

The masterpieces of Paleolithic art, including the cave paintings of Lascaux, France and Altamira, Spain, were produced by Cro-Magnon artists, circa 14,000 B.C. and 9500 B.C. These early painters left images of themselves, as hunters, as well as bears, fish, horses and reindeer, on the walls of caves throughout western Europe. There are no written documents to explain them, but historians believe that the images were made to serve as records or for ritual purposes.

In order to work, the Stone Age artists had to crawl into the recesses of caves, carrying fire, dried sticks, chips of flint, animal fat, earth pigments and bear-hair brushes. Working by firelight, prehistoric painters, like artists of today, used a variety of tools and techniques to produce lines and shading. They drew with charcoal, then applied paint with various implements including their fingers and sticks. Especially clever was their use of hollow bones, through which they blew pigmented paint, an early, yet effective version of the modern-day air-brush.

SOCIAL SCIENCE EXPERIENCE

Concept:

Role specialization has existed from earliest times.

Objective:

To identify the nature of and reasons for role specialization.

Activities:

Discuss the role of the artist from prehistory to today's society.

List some occupations which require the use of specialized tools.

Study examples of prehistoric art.

ART EXPERIENCE

Concept:

When pigment is applied to a textured surface, the image it colors will appear to be softened.

Objectives:

To create a soft-edged image of animals on textured paper, using charcoal and pastel.

To simplify and emphasize contours with a brush line.

To gain skills in shading and control in brushing.

Activity:

Materials: Sandpaper sheets (medium and fine), brushes, a tube of black oil paint, turpentine, charcoal, test paper, pastels in earth colors, chalk, a jar lid.

Directions: On the test paper, use charcoal to lightly sketch outlines of animals.   Make sure the figures are in proportion to one another.   Lay the test paper (drawing side down) over a piece of sandpaper, and rub the back of the test paper to transfer the outlines to the sandpaper. Color the animal shapes on the sandpaper with pastels and shade them with charcoal to show their roundness.   Use the texture of the sandpaper to simulate the fur on the animals.   Squeeze about 1" of black oil paint into the jar lid.   Add enough turpentine to thin the paint enough for it to flow from the brush.   Test the paint on the paper.   Then outline the animals (on the sandpaper) and let everything dry.   Note the differences in edge sharpness/fuzziness between dry media and wet media.

68. TRANSPORT ILLUSTRATORS OF BANGLADESH (B)

In Dhaka, Bangladesh, fossil fuel is in short supply. As a result, people-powered vehicles dominate the private transportation services. Bicycle-driven pedi-cabs and foot-powered rick-shaws are common forms of transportation for hire.

Both kinds of vehicles are carefully (and cleverly) hand-decorated with folkart illustrations and bright blue fabric awnings. Sometimes the subjects depicted are bright and contemporary. However, other illustrations present scenes of war and political upheaval, terrible situations which, unfortunately, are familiar to most of the inhabitants of Dhaka.

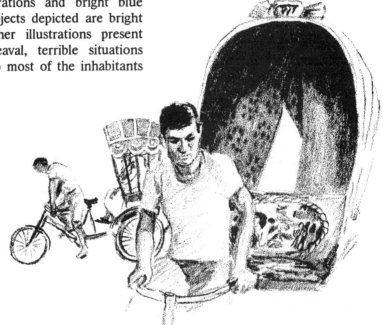

Nevertheless, whatever the subjects may be, the illustrations are all surrounded by frame-like borders. To complete the cabs' decorations, their remaining exterior surfaces are painted with an infinite variety of curvilinear, mostly floral, motifs. As a result, each pedi-vehicle is unique and readily distinguished from all of the thousands of others on the streets of Dhaka.

SOCIAL SCIENCE EXPERIENCE

Concept:

Extreme upheavals in politics influence the customs and art forms of a culture.

Objective:

To identify examples of art and craft applications which reflect the influence of political events.

Activities:

Discuss the ways in which the concerns of governments, organizations, and individuals are reflected in public art.

Research public artworks produced during World War I and World War II.

Discuss the use of public spaces for: propaganda, public service information, advertising, social protest. Make specific references to the posters in Red Square, Moscow; the public monuments in Washington, D.C.; Mexican murals, particularly those of Diego Rivera; American billboards, bus placards, and other forms of public advertising.

Find and cut out pictures of the examples above. Make an exhibit of different forms of public art. Contrast with the concerns of artworks produced for private enjoyment.

Discuss the meaning of "political" and allow students to make observations of a political nature. Analyze the significance of a recent political event.

Study the history of Bangladesh. Discover the other crafts that the people produce; from what resources.

ART EXPERIENCE

Concept:

Dominant (design and color) areas are enhanced by subordinate areas.

Objectives:

To decorate an object with a scene depicting an event in the student's life.

To repeat shapes or simplified motifs from the illustration in a border design.

To develop a dominant color scheme in the illustration and a subordinate one in the border.

To gain skill in designing and painting.

Activity:

Materials: A wooden object (such as a tray, a box, a bookend or some other object to be decorated), acrylic paint, sandpaper, brushes, a water container.

Directions: Select a shape to fit within the surface of the wooden object and design an illustration and border for that shape's dimensions. Sand the wooden object smooth. Paint the object with one of the dominant colors to be used as a background for the illustration. Draw a border around the area of the illustration. Use at least two dominant and two subordinate colors to paint the illustration. Use the second dominant color to paint the border (other minor colors may be used in small amounts, if desired). Allow several successive days to complete the activity.

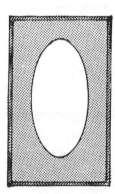  

69. URAMA ISLAND FACE MASKS (B)

Urama is a small island off the southern coast of New Guinea. Its native inhabitants are Papuans whose social order is based on kinship. On Urama, married couples and their daughters live in communal dwellings with other members of their kinship groups, while single men and boys live in separate men's dwellings. These structures are about thirty feet wide and may be hundreds of feet long.

The men of Urama also have ritual houses, called "rave," where ceremonial artifacts, such as shield-like masks, are kept. The colorful masks are believed to represent spirits, and are used to ward off evil spells and bad fortune. Urama masks are long, oval, and tapered at both ends. In the center of each is a stylized skull, often so abstract that the elements of its design are reduced to staring eyes and swirling cheekbones. To non-Papuans, the skulls may look more owl-like than threatening. The shaping of the wooden masks is achieved by burning and by carving with stone tools or shells. To complete their appearance, the masks are painted lime-white, and then decorated with ochres and clays.

SOCIAL SCIENCE EXPERIENCE

Concept:

Rules of grouping by kinship may differ from culture to culture.

Objective:

To learn about systems of kinship.

Activities:

Identify the rules of kinship based on blood relation, marriage, adoption, and others.

List all of the people in your family who form your kinship group.

Study alternate systems, including that of the Papuans and the matrilineal clan system of the Iroquois Indians of (New York and Canada).

Research and make a family tree.

ART EXPERIENCE

Concept:

Symmetrical balance in design is achieved when equal elements appear on both sides of a center point.

Objectives:

To create an abstract, symmetrical design for a face mask in two contrasting colors.

To increase cutting skills.

To learn to work with a mat knife.

Activity:

Materials: Black and white poster board (22" x 28"), a mat knife, scissors, newspapers, white glue, string or elastic, a soft pencil.

Directions: Make a newspaper pattern for an oval mask. Cut a sheet of newsprint to 11" x 28", fold it in half and, then, fold it into quarters.   Draw a curved line from one outside corner to the diagonally opposite corner. Following the drawn line, cut through all four layers. Open out the newsprint into an oval shape. Then, mark and cut eye holes, one on each side of the pattern's vertical center. Trace the oval shaped pattern onto both the black and the white poster boards. Then, cut the boards along the lines. On the back of the black poster board oval, draw a design (around the eye holes), featuring a face or a "skull." Keep symmetry in mind, and make bold patterns. Cut out the design, leaving a black border, and glue the back of the black design to the white oval poster board. (Match up the eye holes.) Punch holes for string or elastic ties to attach the mask to the head or to an arm.

70. NATURE DESIGNS OF MEXICO (B)

The vitality of Mexican painters is perhaps best demonstrated in their painted decoration of common objects. Inspired by nature, they transform such commonplace items as chairs, bowls, spoons and jugs into festively-colored works of art.

Their genius is remarkable. First, they reduce complex decorative motifs, usually based on animal and plant life, to simple, abstract shapes with distinct outlines. Sometimes, the shapes may be somewhat exaggerated or distorted to fit the contours of the surface on which they are to serve as decorations. Likewise remarkable is the ability of the Mexican painters to fill the spaces thus created with balanced, animated designs in which areas of geometric ornamentation are contrasted with texture. The colors are bold and vivid, and the freehand brushwork imparts freshness and vigor to the otherwise common, everyday objects.

SOCIAL SCIENCE EXPERIENCE

Concept:

Native craftspeople use the natural resources of their environment to produce unique designs and crafts.

Objective:

To study the origins and inspirations for folkcraft designs from the students' own environment, and in other regions.

Activities:

Research the plants of Mexico.

Identify the plants and flowers in: Egyptian tomb frescos; Indonesian ikats; Greek geometric period vases; pre-Columbian pottery; and elsewhere.

Collect pictures of animals and plants in the students' local environment to use as a basis for craft designs. Simplify their lines and create motifs.

ART EXPERIENCE

Concept:

Nature's three-dimensional forms can be simplified into two-dimensional shapes.

Objectives:

To decorate a common object with simplified, abstract designs based on animal or plant life.

To reduce the designs to geometric shapes in black and white.

To emphasize shapes by outlining.

To gain skill in design and brushwork.

Activity:

Materials: Art paper, a compass, a ruler, a brush, paint, an object (to be decorated).

Directions: On paper, develop several designs based on animal or plant motifs. Outline the shapes. Exaggerate characteristics and simplify fine details. Fill in the geometric shapes with single brush strokes to indicate textures. Choose designs that best fit the contours of the object to be decorated, and which show the most visual interest in their outlines and patterning. Transfer the designs onto the object to paint. Fill in the spaces around the designs with complimentary but subordinate designs.

71. WALL ART PAINTERS OF HUNGARY (C)

Long ago, Stephen, the first king of Hungary (1001-1038 A.D.) charged that a nation without a past is a nation without a future. Generations of Hungarians have heeded his maxim and have tried to preserve their heritage.   In spite of Hungary's history of recurrent political upheavals, military invasions, damage and destruction, many Hungarian customs continue to survive.

One of the most charming is the traditional "painting party."   Like the American quilting bee or barn-raising, the Hungarian painting party brings friends and neighbors together to accomplish a task: the decoration of the walls of a new home. Designs are based on the colorful motifs to be found in nature. When finished, the wall paintings are permanent, handsome and much cherished by their proud owners.

SOCIAL SCIENCE EXPERIENCE

Concept:

The past is a guide for future plans.

Objective:

To identify and examine the lasting qualities of cultural practices.

Activities:

Discuss the meaning of history and the concept of the individual as a carrier of cultural information. In this light, discuss the importance of education as a way to transmit cultural continuity.

Discuss the reasons for studying history. Examine the idea that a person who carries no cultural information, i.e., a person with no past, is a person with no future.

List other ways that history is recorded: books, recordings, artworks, and more.

List tasks that are more efficiently performed by groups. Design and carry out a task (as a group) that helps a new member or organization in your school or community. Examples: hold a benefit for someone in your community who is ill; paint a mural designed to welcome newcomers to your school; make a quilt for the children's ward of your local hospital.

ART EXPERIENCE

Concept:

Repetition of a motif unifies a design.

Objectives:

To design a wallcovering for a miniature room.

To develop a theme with repeated motifs, colors and shapes.

To gain skills in designing and painting.

Activity:

Materials: A box, tempera paints, a 2" brush, smaller brushes, a ruler.

Directions: Paint the inside of the box with a background color. Use a ruler to draw windows, doors and a cornice (molding). Paint each with a contrasting color. Sketch some related motifs (flowers, natural objects, geometrics) to be used as patterns. Paint (free hand) the interior walls with motifs in a single theme. Each motif may be used as many as three or more times. The spaces between the motifs should be filled with low contrast but related designs. To complete the decor, decorate the rooms with peasant type furniture.

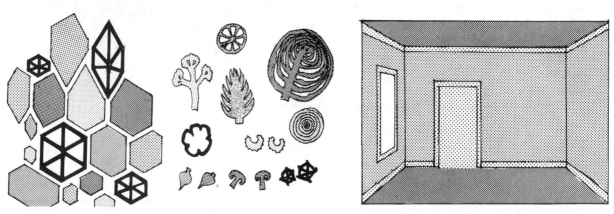

72. SICILY'S ILLUSTRATED CARTS (C)

The island of Sicily has been ruled by Phoenicians, Greeks, Carthaginians, Romans, Saracens, Normans, Byzantines, Armenians, French, Spanish and Italians. In ancient times, during the reign of the Greeks, they described Sicily as a green and beautiful land. However, today Sicily is a poor land, unable to support its native population. Because Sicily's industry is not expanding as rapidly as its population, entire families are forced to emigrate to other Italian cities (or abroad) in the hope of finding employment.

Among those families who are able to earn a living and remain in Sicily are those who practice traditional crafts for sale to neighbors and tourists. One craft, a specialty in Sicily, is the construction and decoration of wooden carts.

Pulled by donkeys, full-sized Sicilian carts are made to carry cargo and passengers. However, the carts come in many sizes, from full-sized down to miniature. Whether it is a work vehicle or a decorative object, the typical Sicilian cart is carved in low relief and painted in lively colors. The illustrations depict figures and scenes, and range from extremely bold to delicately detailed. Especially charming is the fact that when Sicilian carts are moving, their wheels turn into whirls of color. Although modern trucks and automobiles are now used in Sicily, some few craftspeople still remain to construct and decorate Sicily's traditional mode of transportation.

SOCIAL SCIENCE EXPERIENCE

Concept:

The use of traditional craft objects may persist, despite obsolescence, because they perpetuate traditional values and embody meaning for a changing culture.

Objective:

To consider obsolescence: its meaning, causes, effects, advantages, disadvantages.

Activities:

Study the history of Sicily.

Discuss the concept of "exploitation" of people and of resources.

Trace the steps in a region's progression from an agricultural society to an industrial one.

Identify and list the variety of decorations that appear on modes of transportation: lightning bolts on American racing cars, graffiti on subway cars, streamers on bicycle handles, paintings on circus wagons and more.

Design a painted decoration for a mode of transportation. Consider the effects of motion in the design.

Study Pennsylvania Dutch hex signs, Tibetan mandalas, and other examples of radial designs.

ART EXPERIENCE

Concept:

Radial design is balanced in all directions.

Objectives:

To create a radial (wheel-like) design with an emphasis on the center (for use as a hot plate).

To enhance transferring and painting skills.

Activity:

Materials: Paper, a soft pencil, acrylic paint in four colors, brushes, a circle of plywood or heavy cardboard (10" in diameter), scissors.

Directions: Trace the plywood circle pattern onto the paper. Cut out the paper circle. Fold it in half, three times, to create eight wedge-shaped sections. Draw a design on one section. Cut out the section and blacken its back with soft pencil. Transfer the design on the wedge section to the plywood circle, eight times. Paint the design using four colors. Seal the circle with clear acrylic (for use as a hot plate).

73. NAVAJO SAND PAINTING (C)

The Navajo Indians learned the art of sand painting from their Pueblo neighbors and incorporated it into their own tribal ceremonies. To the Navajos, the ritual significance of actually making the sand painting is of primary importance. Aesthetic qualities, while important, are secondary.

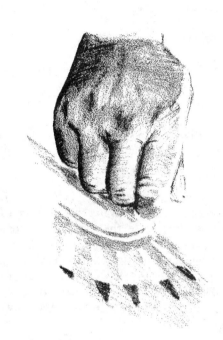

Each Navajo sand painting has a specific meaning and is used for a specific purpose: to heal, to affect weather, to encourage crops. Of the thousand known designs, a Navajo priest may be able to produce somewhere between three and four hundred designs from memory. The ritual prescribes that the designs must be reproduced exactly, and finished within a fixed period of time. It is an unwritten rule that a priest should never attempt to improvise on a design and must always complete in its entirety any design that he starts.

To keep the tradition alive, the priests select talented young apprentices to learn the designs. The knowledge is passed on only by direct teaching and word of mouth. So guarded and sacred is this craft to the Navajos, that only in recent times have the sand painting designs been photographed.

SOCIAL SCIENCE EXPERIENCE

Concept:

Nonliterate societies often have a rich body of traditional lore that is passed on by word of mouth or example.

Objective:

To analyze the phenomenon of tradition: the reasons for its existence, the methods through which it is preserved.

Activities:

Discuss the meaning of word-of-mouth learning.

Consider the reasons why truly "secret" information is not permanently recorded. Discuss the types of information that are kept secret.

Learn about oral histories. Tape record the reminiscences of an older person in your community.

Learn the meanings of various Navajo symbols. Compare Navajo sand paintings to the chalk "veves" of Haitian voodoo priests.

ART EXPERIENCE

Concept:

Three-dimensional forms can be simplified into two-dimensional shapes.

Objectives:

To make a sand painting.

To reduce forms to decorative shapes.

To introduce the skills of cutting stencils and sand painting.

Activity:

Materials: Sandpaper, white glue, a brush, backing cardboard, cans, small bottles, rubber bands, a fine mesh net, a hammer, a sieve, sand, dry pigments, plastic sheets, a stencil, an cutting knife.

Directions: Color sand with dry pigments as follows: In a can, mix 1 part of glue and 1 part of dry color to 2 parts of water and stir in some sand (until it is moistened). Spread out on plastic sheet to dry. Use the hammer to break up any lumps. Then, strain the sand through the sieve and pour it into small bottles. Secure a piece of fine net over the top of each bottle (fasten with rubber bands). Glue sandpaper to the cardboard backing. Cut a stencil for each shape and place the stencils on the sandpaper. One at a time, paint glue through the stencils. Then sprinkle on the color. As each dries, lightly tap off the loose, extra sand. (Repeat for each application of colored sand.) (Also, try applying the glue and pouring the sand without using a stencil.)

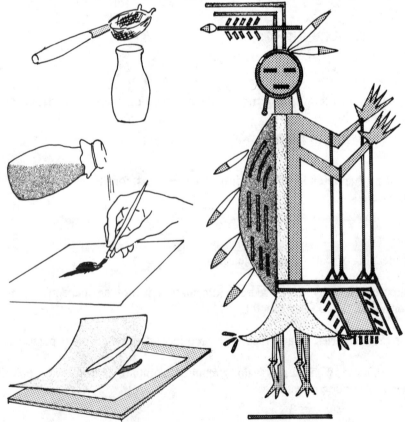

8

CARVE, CUT AND PIERCE

		Level
74)	Chinese Melon Carving.	A
75)	Scriven on Bone	A
76)	Plastic Sculpture.	A
77)	Canadian Inuit Engraving	B
78)	Haida Indian Totems	B
79)	Malaysian Shadow Puppets	B
80)	Decorated Calabashs of Africa	C
81)	Chinese Laquerware	C
82)	Cuna Molas of Panama.	C
83)	Spanish Talabartaria	C
84)	Siberian Bone Carving	C

74. CHINESE MELON CARVING (A)

Perishable materials have long exerted a fascination for artists, as evidenced by the ancient and continuing popularity of such arts as sand painting, flower arranging, topiary, ice carving and sidewalk chalk drawing.   Particularly fascinating is the art of food preparation as practiced by the Chinese.

Traditional Chinese melon carvings serve dual purposes, as both elegant serving vessels and as decorative centerpieces. Carved melons, filled with fragrant meats and vegetables (that have been slowly cooked for many hours), are temptingly displayed on tabletops.   The melons' carved designs often have symbolic meanings. The dragon, for example, stands for good luck. A "good luck" melon decorated with prancing dragons is a traditional centerpiece at Chinese New Year's feasts.

SOCIAL SCIENCE EXPERIENCE

Concept:

Aesthetics (organized beauty) are prized in the Orient (and elsewhere) not only in art works, but also in food preparation.

Objective:

To examine the relationship between economic status and food variety, decoration and symbolism.

Activities:

List art and craft products that are short-lived: Halloween pumpkins, wedding cake decorations, sushi, gingerbread castles, the unrecorded works of performance artists.

Discuss the effects (positive and negative) of photography and audio/video recordings on our memories and experiences.   Consider the objects and events that people choose to record; the effect of the recording on the intensity of people's own recollection of the events.

Gather data about food customs that are said to bring good fortune to people (New Orleans King cake, New Year's fish, black-eyed peas and hog jowls, birthday candles).

ART EXPERIENCE

Concept:

A continuous design leads the eye, without interruption, to the next figure in the pattern.

Objectives:

To carve a melon.

To design a continuous design that leads the eye without interruption to the next figure in the pattern.

To gain skill in carving.

Activity:

Materials: A melon, a small knife, straight pins, a tape measure, paper.

Directions: Measure the circumference of the melon (to determine the length of the design). Plan the design to cover the center half of the melon, leaving the top and the bottom quarters undecorated. Draw a design on paper. Mark where the melon is to be cut above the design, and pin the design paper to the melon. Fit the flat design to the round melon by slitting the design (from its outer edges inward) to conform to the melon's curve. Mark the design with pins and carefully remove the paper, a bit at a time. Scratch in the design's outlines with a sharp pointed knife. Cut away the areas as needed. When finished decorating, cut a saw-tooth edge above the design and to lift off the melon's top. Remove the seeds and/or cut the pulp into serving sized pieces. Replace the pulp or fill the melon with ice, other fruit, vegetable sticks or punch.

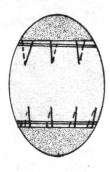  

75. SCRIVEN ON BONE (A)

Cave sites in France, dating from 40,000 to 20,000 B.C., have yielded unique artifacts, such as engraved bones which record the scientific observations of our Paleolithic ancestors. The bones bear drawings that are virtual catalogues of plants and animals, as well as notations about the heavens, especially the waxing and waning of the moon. This evidence of prehistoric record-keeping provides us with a vivid glimpse into the special concerns of early humankind, and proves that ancient people enjoyed a keen eye and a lively intelligence.

The bones were carved with very sharp instruments made of shale, flint or obsidian. Colored dyes and stains made from plants, clays and surface minerals were worked into the engraved grooves in the bone. Although most of the color is no longer visible to the naked eye, it can be seen with a microscope.

SOCIAL SCIENCE EXPERIENCE

Concept:

From earliest times, cultures have invented ways to classify and keep records.

Objective:

To identify the natural modes of human communication; to identify the modern devices that enhance human communication.

Activities:

Discuss the common human need to name, organize and recognize relationships between cause and effect in the natural world.

Study systems of naming and organizing: the systems of Linnaeus, Dewey (Decimal), the Library of Congress; the aisles in a supermarket; the parking lots at a large mall or stadium.

Collect pictures of the natural world and classify their subject content.

ART EXPERIENCE

Concept:

Line describes the contour of objects.

Objectives:

To make an engraving in plaster of an animal or plant.

To color the grooves to contrast them against the white of the plaster.

To practice incising technique.

Activity:

Materials: A metal stylus or nail, a pint-sized plastic bowl (butter or margarine container) or a short length of plastic pipe, some plaster of paris, color from natural sources (petals, leaves, clay), a wooden block, a cotton swab, a "C" clamp.

Directions: Pour plaster of Paris into the bowl (or pipe length) a day or two before work is to begin. Collect sources of color. Make drawings on paper that are larger in scale than the engraving is to be. Remove the plaster from the bowl (pipe). Clamp the wooden block to the table and brace the plaster against it. Transfer the drawing to the plaster. Then, hold the stylus firmly and cut short grooves in the lines of the design. Keep the hands away from the front of the cutting tool. When the incising of the design is complete and the grooves are deep enough to hold color, make a paste of the color and work it into the grooves with the cotton swab. Wipe away the extra color. To make a print, cover the design with a thin layer of paint, then press (or roll) onto a piece of paper, cloth or a wooden surface.

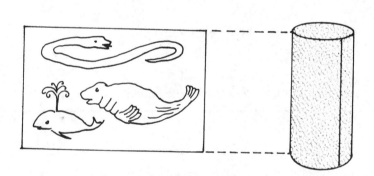  

76. AMERICAN PLASTIC SCULPTURE (A)

Plastics are synthetic materials derived from petroleum. When exposed to heat, they become malleable and can be molded into any shape. After the heat is removed, the plastic will cool and will keep its shape. Many varieties of plastics have been developed and put to innumerable uses, such as packaging and containers, the mechanical and structural parts of machines and appliances, eyeglass lenses and surgical gloves, computer disks and frying pan coatings. The diversity of plastic materials, and the ease of their manipulation and coloration, has made them almost indispensible.

Because artists and craftspeople have always exploited new materials, it is not surprising that they have found many uses for plastics. Some previously used plastics can be reworked after exposure to heat. Most can be drilled, doweled or gouged. Lightweight, yet strong, plastic threads can tie object to object, while sheets of plastic can be formed into almost every imaginable construction. With so many variations, plastics are among the most versatile, practical and popular media available to sculptors today.

SOCIAL SCIENCE EXPERIENCE

Concept:

Craftspeople create crafts with whatever materials are at hand.

Objective:

To identify the benefits and liabilities connected with the use of plastic.

Activities:

Consider life without plastics. List items that were formerly made from other materials that are now made of plastic.

Discuss the environmental problems associated with the use of plastics, i.e., no decay, the emission of fumes when burned.

Study the work of artists who use plastics: George Segal, Dwayne Hansen, Red Grooms.

Learn about the basic types of plastic, how they are made, and how they can be worked.

ART EXPERIENCE

Concept:

Forms have convex, concave and flat planes.

Objectives:

To make a plastic sculpture.

To create a three-dimensional figure from a two-dimensional plastic sheet.

To turn a flat shape into a dynamic form.

To develop skill in cutting heavy plastic material; also, bending, twisting and forming.

Activity:

Materials: Thermoplastic sheet, a frying pan or toaster oven, aluminum foil, scissors, gloves or pot holders, pliers, a nail or an awl.

Directions: Develop the shape of a figure on paper and use it as a pattern. Scratch or trace the pattern onto the plastic sheet. Heat the plastic in a foil-lined pan (at 350° F. for 1/2 hour, or until the plastic begins to be pliable). Handle it with gloves and cut along scratched lines with scissors. If the plastic begins to harden, return it to the heat until it softens. Form a simple sculpture. (If desired, leave a tab at the bottom, to mount in a "slit block" for display.)

77. CANADIAN INUIT ENGRAVING (B)

Most of the Canadian Arctic has been explored.   Usually the purpose of the exploration was to find land and minerals for exploitation.   However, some explorers strove to make observations about the daily lives of Inuits and to record their ways.

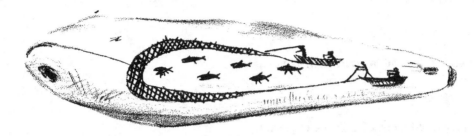

Traders and whalers followed in the footsteps of the early expeditions, bringing new goods and materials to the Arctic, and in turn, popularizing Inuit folk arts and crafts in the world at large.

All of this contact with outsiders has changed Inuit life (some say for the better, others, for the worse).   The outsiders taught the Inuits how to do scrimshaw, ropework, stone carving and basketry.   They brought tools and materials to the Inuits and provided a ready market for their finished work.   Examples of Inuit art soon found their way into museums around the world.

The everyday objects decorated before 1900 tell us the most about the original Inuit way of life.   Bone handles for spoons and knives, wooden paddles, spear points and stone weights for fishnets were engraved with various scenes depicting tribespeople at work.   The lines scratched into walrus ivory, bone, stone and wood were darkened by applying a mixture of dark pigment and fat, then wiping the excess mixture off of the smooth surfaces.   Sometimes designs were tinted with natural colors to suggest forms and textures.

SOCIAL SCIENCE EXPERIENCE

Concept:

Contact between divergent cultures and the availability of natural resources can influence the methods and styles of craft production.

Objectives:

To identify the resources of the Inuit before contact with other cultures.   To compare these findings with the resources made available after outside contact occurred.

Activities:

Discuss the influence of trade on an economy with limited resources.

Suggest ways in which new trade goods, materials and tools would change the lifestyle of people in a remote culture.

Study Inuit art and culture, past and present.

Study the stories of the Arctic explorers.

Research and write a play based on an Inuit myth.

ART EXPERIENCE

Concept:

Incised design is enhanced by contrast in value.

Objectives:

To make an engraved scene of daily life in plaster.

To emphasize a dominant figure through scale and textural detail.

To define lines and shapes by rubbing in contrasting pigment.

To increase skill in incising and carving.

To learn safety rules.

Activity:

Materials: 1/2 lb. of plaster of Paris, a small aluminum pie pan (or a tall, 32 oz. can), dark shoe polish, nails or engraving tools, a soft cloth, grease, a bucket, wooden blocks, "C" clamps.

Directions: In the bucket, mix the plaster with water to a creamy thickness.   Then, pour some into the greased pie pan (or the tall can).   Leave the plaster container to dry for two or three days and remove it from the container.   Then, let the plaster dry for another two days.   Meanwhile, sketch a scene of everyday life.   Include figures and animals, if desired. Make a major figure the most detailed and prominent in size.   Blacken the back of the sketch and transfer its design by tracing it onto the surface of the pie pan plaster (or onto the plaster cylinder formed by the can).   Clamp the plaster to the table between wooden blocks.   Use the nails (or engraving tools) to incise the design, being careful to keep hands behind the direction of the scratch.   When the design is complete, use a soft cloth to rub some dark wax into the lines, to bring out the design's features.

78. HAIDA INDIAN TOTEMS (B)

Totem poles are comparatively new to the Haida Indians of British Columbia. The idea for them may have been borrowed from the Polynesians, who, long ago, traveled from far across the Pacific in their canoes. The totem pole probably is an adaptation of the carved house poles that are situated at the entranceways to Haida houses. In time, free-standing, elaborately carved poles were developed. Other northwest tribes, such as the Tlingit and Tsimishian Indians, also made totem poles, but the Haida of Queen Charlotte Island have been especially noted for their craftsmanship.

The figures that appear on Haida totem poles, such as ravens, wolves, frogs, eagles, halibut, owls and deer, are not fetishes or gods; rather, they are a system of native heraldry, family symbols that indicate ancestry and tribal organization. The tallest wooden totem in the Queen Charlotte area is 81 feet high.

Today, the Haida prefer to work in argillite, a clay-like rock, partly because of the shortage of wood, but also because stone carvings are more easily marketed. Details carved into argillite will be more durable than is the wood in the aged and decaying totems that stand, gray and pitted from wind and rain, on the sandy beaches of Queen Charlotte.

A new full-sized totem stretches its wings wide in the Haida meeting house. Its many carved eyes watchover the present workings of the tribe.

SOCIAL SCIENCE EXPERIENCE

Concept:

Cultures adopt the techniques and materials of other cultures, but usually adapt them to their own motifs.

Objective:

To learn about Haida culture, the custom of the potlatch, and the clan system.

Activities:

Make a list of the states and countries from which students' parents and grandparents came. Assign a symbolic animal to each place. Design totem poles based on the symbolic animals assigned to each students' origins.

Research the totem poles of the Northwest Coast Indians and the carvings by Polynesians. Discuss the uses to which wood from trees lends itself in both of these cultures. Discuss totem poles, canoes and more.

Compare the economy and lifestyle of the Haida and/or other northwest native Americans, as they were 100 years ago and as they are today.

ART EXPERIENCE

Concept:

Similar forms create harmony.

Objectives:

To carve a totem pole.

To create harmony and monumentality by repetition of simplified forms.

To increase skills in simplifying, carving, constructing and painting.

To practice safety procedures.

Activity:

Materials: 2 balsawood blocks (one, 9" x 2" x 2" and another, 8" x 2" x 1/4"), a mat knife, a coping saw, sandpaper, glue, clear plastic spray, tempera paint, a pencil, tracing paper and a "C" clamp.

Directions: Trace the outlines of the sides of the 9" x 2" wooden blocks onto the tracing paper and draw designs for totem figures, to size within the outlines. Simplify and compress the figures. Draw all four side views, plus the bottom and the top. Lay the side views on top of one another to check their proportions (and make sure they match). Transfer the finished drawings to the block. Fasten the block to the table with a "C" clamp. Cut away nonessential edges, working symmetrically.   Make sure the direction of the cuts is away from the hands and body. Use the coping saw to cut curves, profiles and also wing pieces, if desired. Make slits into the totem to fit the wings. When the carving is complete, glue the wings and support them, until the glue is dry. Paint in tempera colors and spray with clear plastic.

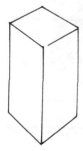

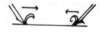

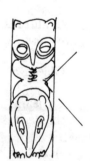

79. MALAYSIAN SHADOW PUPPETS (B)

Shadow puppets in plays are as familiar to the people in Malaysia as animated cartoons are to people in the West. The puppets are visual stereotypes that portray traditional characters from myths and fables, as well as immediately recognizable caricatures of people in occupational and cultural situations. Gods and "good" characters have almond-shaped eyes, small pointed noses and graceful figures. Evil demons have round, bulging eyes, and distorted noses and bodies.

Traditional shadow puppets are made of tanned hides. The flexible body parts are tied together at the joints with cord. Bamboo sticks are attached to the ends of each limb and are manipulated by skilled puppeteers, to simulate movement. The importance of each puppet in the play is indicated by the degree of complexity in its pierced design, and thus, in the enhanced details of the shadow it throws.

Typical of these shadow puppets are those portraying the Dog of Fo, a Malaysian demon, popular and frightening to the audience and thought to be responsible for minor disasters. In China, where they are called "Fu Dogs," or "Lion Dogs," they are considered an omen of death.

SOCIAL SCIENCE EXPERIENCE

Concept:

Nonliterate (or semiliterate) cultures often have a rich body of traditional lore that is passed on by rituals and word of mouth.

Objective:

To recognize and analyze nonliterate communication methods and media; in the world at large and in one's own life.

Activities:

Discuss the history of puppetry, theater and pageantry, as methods of imparting an oral tradition to a culture.

Study the shadow puppets of Indonesia.

Watch a film or a videotape of an Indonesian shadow puppet play. Compare the performance to: a Thanksgiving play, a Punch and Judy (or other) puppet show, a Saturday morning cartoon show.

Write a play for shadow figures.

Make an exhibit of hand puppets, stick puppets and marionettes.

ART EXPERIENCE

Concept:

The patterning of areas suggests textures.

Objectives:

To make a shadow puppet.

To simplify the puppet's silhouette.

To create a pattern or texture through the repetition of pierced holes.

To define contour by piercing design lines.

To consider the possibilities of movement in designing a jointed figure.

To practice skills of piercing, cutting and punching.

Activity:

Materials: Tagboard or pie tin metal, a hole punch or a hammer and a nail, wood, pliers, shears (or a mat knife), clothes hangers, a wire cutter, tape, 3/4 inch cotter pins (or paper clips), a single light source.

Directions: Sketch a puppet, including plans for piercing and jointing. Trace the puppet design onto metal (or tagboard). Cut out the parts. Pierce the designs by tapping a nail through the metal (or board) into the wood. (A hole punch will work on tagboard.) Assemble the pieces and connect them with cotter pins or paper clips. Tape coat hanger wire to the ends of the puppet's limbs and to the back of its body. Place a strong light behind the puppet to cast its shadow on a wall or screen.

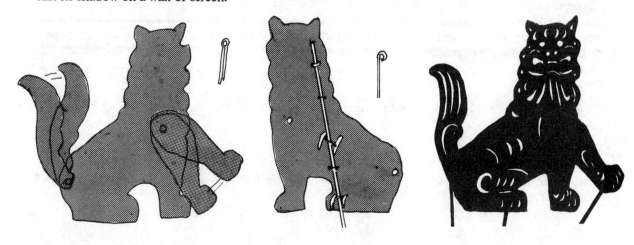

80. DECORATED CALABASHS OF AFRICA (C)

The African calabash, a versatile gourd, is perfectly suited to the needs of both the crafts-person and the householder. Well-known in Nigeria, Niger, Dahomey, Cameroon and the Congo, the calabash grows on a thick, climbing vine and is related to the squash, pumpkin and cucumber. Its dried shell is hard and lightweight, with a smooth, even surface that is ideal for carving. The calabash grows in many shapes and sizes that are just right for making into bowls, ladles, cups, dishes, ink pots, bottles, and many other useful items.

Often given as a bridal gift, a decorated calabash signifies wealth and status and is highly cherished by its owner. The artist works directly on the gourd, carving bold geometric shapes and folkloric symbols such as highly-stylized suns, snakes, birds and animals into its surface. First, using the curved blade of a knife, a pattern is outlined on a gourd. Then, the background is cut away to leave the decorative design in low relief and darker than the natural background. In another technique, the design may be burned into the surface of the calabash with a hot knife. Painting is used in both techniques to enhance the contrasts of the design.

SOCIAL SCIENCE EXPERIENCE

Concept:

Cultures with few natural resources make extensive use of materials that are available.

Objective:

To identify various natural items that are adapted for use as tools or utensils.

Activities:

Study the African cultures who use calabash utensils. Suggest uses and limitations for a calabash utensil.

Discuss traditional bridal gifts in our own and other cultures. List some examples of domestic items we often give as bridal gifts. Which ones signify status?

Gather data on the geographic areas and climate where calabashes can be grown.

Find (and classify as to the degree and kind of adaptation involved) other examples of natural materials used to make utensils. Bring examples of the example items to school (wooden spoons and salad bowls, woven raffia place mats, straw whisk brooms and more), or find pictures of them for a board display.

ART EXPERIENCE

Concept:

High value contrast is most dramatic.

Objectives:

To decorate a gourd.

To create a repeated geometric design.

To use dramatic contrast between the gourd's natural color and the applied decoration.

To improve skill in brushwork and learn woodburning techniques.

Activity:

Materials: Gourds, rubber bands, a pencil, a brush, India ink, a coping saw. Optional: a woodburning tool.

Directions: To prepare a fresh gourd, cut off its top (the area surrounding its stem). Reserve to use as a lid (if desired). Scoop out the meat, then, fill the gourd with water to rot out its seeds. Drain and thoroughly dry. Cut the gourd to its desired shape. Then decorate it with a repeating geometric design. (Draw horizontal lines by tracing along rubber bands that are stretched around the gourd.) Carefully paint or burn designs onto gourd. If more color is desired, the background can be dyed with a natural dye.

81. CHINESE LACQUERWARE (C)

Chinese artisans have used lacquer to protect and decorate their craft objects from the days of the Han dynasty (second century B.C.) to the present. Europeans once believed that the lacquer used by Oriental artists was an artificial product made according to a secret formula. However, Chinese lacquer actually is a natural product that comes from the lac tree that grows in both China and Japan. Today, everyone can use lacquer because several synthetic types have been formulated and are in use all over the world.

Traditional Chinese lacquer artists use the same painstaking techniques as did their ancestors to construct beautiful and costly dishes, boxes and chests. They apply coat after coat of lacquer, sometimes forty or more coats, to thin wooden boxes until a smooth finish is achieved. Traditional lacquer colors are black, red, dark green and gold. White and other colors are used sparingly, mostly for highlighting. Lacquerware is likely to last for a long time. The vibrant colors of Han dynasty pieces, buried for some 2,000 years, are as intense as those that are produced today.

SOCIAL SCIENCE EXPERIENCE

Concept:

The value of an art or craft object is determined by many criteria, including: the base worth of the materials used, the amount of time/skill/labor involved in its creation, its rarity, its aesthetic value, and its historic place.

Objective:

To identify the criteria which would determine the value of each art and/or craft item in this chapter.

Activities:

Study the uses and limitations of natural lacquer. Compare with the uses of today's synthetic lacquers.

Compare pictures of Han Dynasty and other antique lacquerware with today's boxes, dishes and chests.

Compare the mass-produced lacquer objects of the 20th century with older, one of a kind examples of similar pieces.

ART EXPERIENCE

Concept:

Radial balance fits the round format.

Objectives:

To make a "lacquered" bowl or box with a decoration designed to fit its shape.

To apply mold-making techniques to papier-mache.

To gain skill in smoothing, sanding, cutting and painting.

Activity:

Materials: A bowl or a box (disposable, for use as a mold), newsprint, paste, clear acrylic paint, acrylic paints in colors, brushes, scissors, sandpaper.

Directions: Tear the newsprint into 1" strips.   Soak some of the strips in water.   Turn the bowl (or box) upside down and cover it with a layer of wet newsprint strips.   Dip the remainder of the newsprint strips in water-based paste.   Then, cover the bowl with at least four complete layers of pasted strips.   (Apply them in alternating directions.)   Smooth all of the layers. When dry, remove the hardened layers and trim their edges neatly.   Sand the inside.   Next, paint the paper bowl black, red or dark green.   Set it aside to dry.   Cover the paint with two coats of clear acrylic.   Paint on designs.   Then, finish by applying three coats of clear acrylic.

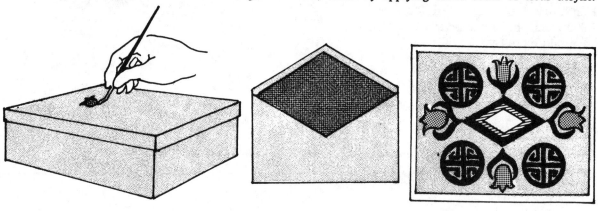

82. CUNA MOLAS OF PANAMA (C)

The country of Panama has had a stormy history with many changes in its government. Today it is independent, but for a long time, the government of Panama and its most important geographic feature, the Panama Canal, were controlled by the United States.

The Panama Canal cuts through the isthmus of Panama for 51 miles and connects the Atlantic and Pacific Oceans. Because of its international importance, Panama and the Panama Canal Zone have attracted residents from all over the world. Although the majority of the population speak Spanish and many speak English, there are also native Indian tribes who maintain their own languages and customs.

Among the best known of these are the Cuna, who inhabit the San Blas islands on the Atlantic side of the country. The Cuna maintain their cultural and political independence by deliberately keeping their contact with the outside world at a minimum.

Cuna craftspeople carve balsawood and mahogany products for sale to traders and tourists. But they are best known as the originators of the "mola," an applique' made of sewn layers of fabric. Molas usually have natural, animal or bird, motifs and are constructed of an upper layer of cloth, from which pieces are cut out, according to the design, and a lower layer, onto which the cut layer is sewn. The final effect allows the under-fabric to show through the upper-fabric's cut outs.

Traditional mola designs were originally painted directly onto the body. However, in the 16th century, the arrival of Spanish missionaries (with their insistence on clothing the body), soon put an end to this practice. Happily, the original designs were not forgotten and were adapted for use in fabric design.

Today, Cuna women compete to see who can create the most intricate and innovative designs. Blouses, shirts and skirts show the plant life, snakes, turtles and other creatures found in the Cuna environment. Also, since their contact with the modern world has increased, Cuna designers have begun to use some modern motifs, such as airplanes and ocean liners. Trading companies now market molas for sale in galleries, stores and museums.

SOCIAL SCIENCE EXPERIENCE

Concept:

Cultures tend to retain parts of their own traditions, despite changes that occur due to contact with other cultures.

Objective:

To examine the ways in which a simple culture can absorb new stimuli and products to their advantage.

Activities:

Create a fabric design that would also work as a tattoo or body painting.

Study examples of body decoration and hair ornamentation from other cultures: Japanese tattooing, 17th century French wigs, African hair weaving.

Find pictures of 16th century Spanish missionaries and consider their appearance to the Cuna, and vice versa. Discuss other effects the Spanish conquistadors had on Indian populations of Central and South America.

Make an exhibit of pictures of unusual costumes and fashions throughout history.

ART EXPERIENCE

Concept:

Complexity is built by the repetition of subordinate patterns.

Objectives:

To create a mola-style design.

To simplify the shape of a bird or animal as the dominant motif.

To add complexity with subordinate patterns built from contrasting layers of color within the motif.

To enhance the features of the feathers, fur markings or scales through repetition of textural patterns.

To increase skill in cutting.

Activity:

Materials: Four 9" x 12" sheets of fadeless paper in contrasting colors, scissors or a mat knife, rubber cement, a pencil, heavy cardboard.

Directions: On the back of the darkest-colored sheet, draw a 1" border as a frame for the picture. Draw the simplified outline of an animal or bird, leaving a 1/2" border around it. Connect the outline of the figure to the border on all four sides with several 1/4"-wide bands. Be sure that any divisions within the figure are similarly connected to its outline. (If a mat knife is to be used for cutting, work on top of cardboard.) Cut out the spaces between the lines, taking care not to sever the connecting bands. Place the second sheet under the cut sheet and cut inside each space, leaving a 1/8" border all the way around. Repeat with the third sheet. If the spaces are too large, divide them so that all spaces at this level are no more than 1" square in area. Do not cut the last (fourth) sheet. Glue all of the layers together.

 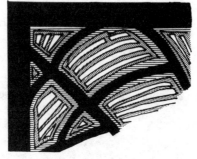 

83. SPANISH TALABARTERIA (C)

In Spain, leatherwork is called "talabarteria," after leather belts called "talabartes" to which swords were once strapped. Spanish leatherworkers are noted for their decorative, useful leather products: bridles and harnesses, chaps and leggings, aprons, suitcases, purses and boots. They are masters of leatherworking techniques, including braiding, tooling and pierced decoration.

The artisans of Toledo and Avila in central Spain are specially admired for their fine leather cutouts, known as openwork. Usually made of lightweight leather, some openwork garments can be as much as four layers thick at the seams. The bottom layer of leather is usually white, while the covering layers range from tan to deep brown (although some may be dyed with other colors).

SOCIAL SCIENCE EXPERIENCE

Concept:

The value of an art and craft object is determined by many criteria, including: the base worth of the materials used, the amount of time/skill/labor involved in its creation, its rarity, its aesthetic value, and its historic place.

Objective:

To examine the criteria that affect value.

Activities:

Find examples of cultural change that have resulted in utilitarian objects being more valued for aesthetic reasons than for their usefulness (American country crafts, telephone pole insulators, stained glass windows).

Learn about the Spanish leather industry.

Invite a local leatherworker to speak to your class about different types of leather and leatherworking techniques.

ART EXPERIENCE

Concept:

Repetition unifies in a high contrast design.

Objectives:

To make a pouch, case or book cover that is decorated with Spanish-style openwork.

To create a unified, high contrast design through repetition of shape.

To gain skill in sewing and cutting.

Activity:

Materials: Felt or lightweight leather in a dark and a light color, a hole punch, scissors, a needle and thread (or fabric glue), pins, a pattern (for the item—a pouch, a case, a book cover—to be decorated).

Directions: Pin the pattern to the light-colored material and cut it out.   Measure the area where the decoration will be, and cut out the dark material to the same size. Draw the design in chalk on the back of the dark material. In the case of a very open design, staple the dark material (leather or felt) to heavy paper for extra support. Next, cut or punch holes where noted in the design. Allow enough space (about every 1") to sew the dark piece to the light material. The outside edges of the dark piece may be sewn into the seam or sawtoothed, as a decorative border around the edge. Sew the dark piece to the light and then sew the item together.

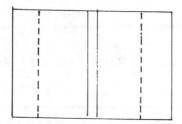  

84. SIBERIAN BONE CARVING (C)

Winter in Siberia lasts for seven months, from October to April. The temperature may drop to 40 or 60 degrees F. below zero, keeping children from going to school and their parents from their work. Heavy snows and ice blanket the land, and only the hardiest of people can risk leaving their snug homes to go elsewhere.

During these dark months, it is the tradition for Siberian artisans to use the bones and teeth they have collected during the hunting season to carve figurines and articles for summer sales. A primary source of ivory-like material is whale teeth which are not as large as elephant tusks, but are of such fine quality that they allow for the use of greater detail in carved work. Also carved are the tusks of walruses and seals, as well as the bones of musk-ox and other large mammals. Many Siberian carvings depict, besides animals, human figures engaged in local occupations. In Tobolsk, the folkart carvings depict ancestors, herdsmen, dogs, deer, musk-ox and walrus.

SOCIAL SCIENCE EXPERIENCE

Concept:

Work patterns are influenced by geography, weather and available resources.

Objective:

To identify the effects of environment on human behaviors.

Activities:

Locate Siberian and Tobolsk in the U.S.S.R. Identify the geographic and climatic influences on Siberian carving as they affect both materials and work patterns.

Study the history of the whaling industry. Learn about the walrus, seal and narwhal.

ART EXPERIENCE

Concept:

Organic forms are derived from geometric forms.

Objectives:

To carve an animal or human figure from a bar of soap.

To maintain balance and a sense of the basic geometric form by designing a figure that touches all six sides of the soap bar.

To develop skill in subtractive sculpture.

To add interest with texture and details.

Activity:

Materials: A bath-sized, rectangular bar of soap, plastic knives, nails, paper clips, a felt-tip marker, paper, a pencil.

Directions: Make sketches of the figure to be carved, from its top, bottom, sides, front and rear.   Study the sketches.   Make sure some part of the figure touches each face of the soap bar.   Draw all sides of the figure—to size—on the paper, and using the marker, transfer the lines to the bar of soap.   Working from the largest to the smallest forms, cut away the unneeded parts of the soap.   Reserve cutting between the legs (and around the tail, if any) until the last.   Finish the figure with textural details of fur, scales, hide or clothing.

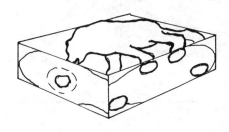 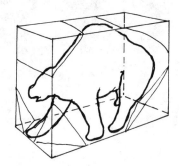 

NOTES

NOTES

NOTES

NOTES

NOTES

NOTES

NOTES